A CHANGED MAN

It happened in 1971, in a Holiday Inn, of all places. The other band members and road crew were checking into their rooms down the hall as John closed the door and collapsed on the double bed. As had become his custom, John began to pray to a God he did not really know but had come to believe in. Almost imperceptibly, his silent, interior meditation became an audible, vocal question: "Lord, who are you?"

Then it happened . . .

John was never the same after that evening at the Holiday Inn. He nourished the budding new life within by even more intensive Bible study and deeper times of meditative prayer. But love is hard to hide, and before long those around him felt its warmth. They could see that something had changed. "I think they could see the acceptance, the simple love, and the forgiveness that had become the driving forces of my life," he says. "I was in the midst of a conversion."

DAN O'NEILL

TROUBADOUR FOR THE LORD

The Story of
John Michael Talbot

BANTAM BOOKS
TORONTO · NEW YORK · LONDON · SYDNEY · AUCKLAND

This low-priced Bantam Book
has been completely reset in a type face
designed for easy reading, and was printed
from new plates. It contains the complete
text of the original hard-cover edition.
NOT ONE WORD HAS BEEN OMITTED.

TROUBADOUR FOR THE LORD

A Bantam Book / published by arrangement with
Crossroad/Continuum Publishing Company

PRINTING HISTORY
Crossroad edition published June 1983
Bantam edition / December 1987

ISBN 0-553-26900-3

Published simultaneously in the United States and Canada

Bantam Books are published by Bantam Books, Inc. Its trade-
mark, consisting of the words "Bantam Books" and the por-
trayal of a rooster, is Registered in U.S. Patent and Trademark
Office and in other countries. Marca Registrada. Bantam
Books, Inc., 666 Fifth Avenue, New York, New York 10103.

PRINTED IN THE UNITED STATES OF AMERICA

O   0 9 8 7 6 5 4 3 2 1

*This book is dedicated to
Saint Francis of Assisi, to the
Little Portion House of Prayer,
and to all who have followed
in the footsteps of Saint Francis*

Contents

Acknowledgments

I wish to thank the following people who have been vital to the process of writing this manuscript: Cherry O'Neill; Ed Durst; Father Michael J. Schmitt; Bishop Bernard F. Law; Father Martin Wolter, O.F.M.; Michael Leach; Cheri White; and Ted Terry. Special thanks also go to the Talbot family for their cooperation.

Preface

The troubadours were itinerant lyric poets and musicians who flourished in Europe from the eleventh through the thirteenth century. They wandered throughout the continent, particularly in southern France, northern Italy, and eastern Spain. Their rhymes were usually love songs, and most of these medieval minstrels composed their own material. It was not uncommon for them to have noble blood in their veins—they were the upper-class, establishment dropouts of their era.

Giovanni Francesco Bernardone was just such a person. He was born the son of a wealthy cloth merchant in the Italian town of Assisi in about 1182. Francis, as he was later to be called, opted out of the status quo as the result of a profound religious conversion experience. Donning a ragged cloak of sackcloth belted with a length of rope, he proceeded to incite a peaceful "overthrow" of Europe in a gentle revolution of love. The intriguing tales of Saint Francis of Assisi have filled the hearts and imaginations of men for nearly eight hundred years and have become incarnate in the lives and works of a worldwide movement, the Order of Friars Minor, or the Franciscans, in all its diverse forms and expressions.

Today Saint Francis's spiritual revival continues, not only within the traditional ranks of lay and religious Franciscans, but in a growing atmosphere of social awakening, ecumenical dialogue, and international spiritual renewal. A growing number of Christian pilgrims are walking in the footsteps of a truly legendary figure, committing themselves to the radical Gospel expression of love as exemplified by the life of Saint Francis, one of our Lord's most dynamic and colorful disciples.

One such individual is John Michael Talbot, now a Franciscan monk. Talbot, a former pop musician, captures the true spirit of Franciscan spirituality; from his brown habit to his inspiring music, he bears the unmistakable marks of a modern-day troubadour. He has offered up his entire life and prodigious talent to God. His story will inspire you.

Chapter One

A Musical Inheritance

It was March 27, 1982. I landed at the Sacramento airport, hastily rented a car, and smiled to myself as I drove to Saint Ignatius Catholic Church. I'll be early, I thought, with the certainty of one who likes compulsive, detailed planning. Wrong. As I turned into the expansive church parking lot there was not a slot to be found, and a dozen other drivers were cruising for spaces. My first surprise at a John Michael Talbot concert was being unable to find a parking place, even though I had arrived ninety minutes early.

As the late-afternoon mass concluded at Saint Ignatius, a swelling crowd clamored at several entrances in eager anticipation. Unlike other religious concerts I had attended, this one was attracting an audience much more diverse than the predictably youthful following of most contemporary Christian performers. Small children, teens, collegiates, married couples and senior citizens created a kind of extended-family atmosphere, complete with a generous sprinkling of priests and nuns who speckled the crowd with black-and-white habits and clerical collars. I began to sense a contagious quality of expectation and excitement.

Tucked discreetly away in an adjacent building, John Talbot was directing the final rehearsal with the one-hundred-voice choir. Of course, I eavesdropped. Crouching in a corner I observed John as he orchestrated several of the evening's upcoming numbers. A tenor leaned over and whispered nervously in my ear, "We've been practicing a whole year for this single night!" Now, that's commitment—no wonder they sounded so good.

As the big moment approached, John led the singers in a hushed, brief prayer. "Lord Jesus, lead us, direct us, minister through us in the creative, spontaneous power of Your Holy Spirit. Make us instruments of Your peace. In the name of the Father, the Son, and the Holy Spirit, amen." Now I was fully caught up in the flow of the event. For me, the concert had already begun.

John slung his guitar over his back and shuffled toward me with a grin on his bearded face. "It's about time you caught one of these concerts, Dan. I think you'll really enjoy it." He looked every inch the Franciscan monk, with the hooded dark-brown habit draped over his tall, lean frame. He fiddled unconsciously with the knotted white rope that traditionally belts the garment of the disciples of Saint Francis and continued, "I have reserved a front-row seat for you."

In my excellent vantage point in the sanctuary of the spacious church, I produced a pen and paper to record my impressions. A full half hour before the start of the concert, the place was packed—even standing room was gone and hundreds were being turned away at the door. All eyes were riveted on the empty stage when John emerged to test the microphones. Applause burst forth spontaneously. "Testing . . . testing one, two, testing."

"Oooh! His voice sounds just like on his records!" a teenage girl squealed. "And he looks even better than on the album jacket." Obviously this guy has dedicated fans, I noted to myself. People even love his sound checks! John joked with those in the first few rows as he tuned his guitar.

As the house lights gradually faded to a dim glow, silence cloaked the hall. The melodious notes of a skillfully played instrument suddenly filled the air and a long, narrow shaft of light pierced the darkness, falling on the diminutive robed figure who leaned into the microphone with closed eyes and uplifted face.

"Sing hallelujah to the Wonderful Counselor . . . ," the voice drifted through the place like sweet incense. More than eighteen hundred listeners hung on every word, every note, until the song concluded, then roared in unrestrained approval. Flashbulbs and strobes popped by the score.

"I hope you didn't come here this evening to be entertained. I left that business about ten years ago." Smiling, he paused a moment and urged, "Let us enter into the presence of God in song. Saint Augustine said, 'He who sings well, prays twice.'" The throng joined in with enthusiasm in a round of "Sing Hallelujah." It sounded like heaven—a truly amazing experience.

At the end of his first song John paused, rolled up his loose brown sleeves, propped his bare feet on a rung of the stool on which he was perched, and explained, "Singing is really a form of prayer. It demonstrates unity when we all join together in this collective act of prayerful worship. Let's reflect on this as we continue our worship together this evening." He bowed his head in supplication, hands folded.

Silent moments passed. Then his fingers once again danced deftly across the strings of his simple guitar with expert precision. Melodious songs of praise flowed effortlessly and he captivated the audience through his gentle, endearing manner. He sang "Holy Is His Name," "The Lilies of the Field," and, of course, the timeless "Peace Prayer of Saint Francis."

"In my more contemplative moments I often visualize my life as though it were an empty canvas. I envisage Jesus as a master painter. We can become something beautiful—the creative work of his infinitely skilled hands." John launched into "Empty Canvas" from his album *The Painter,* an apparent favorite of many in the audience.

Then, the grand finale—songs from John's bestselling album *The Lord's Supper,* complete with the one-hundred-voice choir. "We Shall Stand Forgiven" was followed by "Glory to God in the Highest," at which point the place exploded into high praise and boundless, jubilant worship. The hall was electrified by the sound of nearly two thousand voices. I had never seen anything quite like this—it was almost Pentecostal, yet somehow tempered by Catholic restraint and order.

John spoke with a kind of hushed, firm confidence. "You know, we would all represent an incredible force for peace if we would just unite and take our faith seriously. The revolution must begin inside—in our hearts! I am speaking of a gentle revolution, free as the wind—you can't see it, but this awesome energy is all around us in the power of the Spirit."

Finally, at John's request we stood and joined hands, singing the Lord's Prayer. I later wrote in my journal that this was a "salient moment of pure spiritual vitality, made tangible by the human linkage of hands and hearts."

Most of the throng filed out of the church on a spiritual high, while a remaining hundred or so rushed the stage, hoping for a photo, an autograph, or perhaps a word or two with the Franciscan brother who had had such immense impact that evening. It took me more than an hour to extricate John from the place.

"Well, what do you think? Did it go okay? How about the choir, did their voices project?" John asked anxiously, seemingly unaware of his great success. "All I want is to bring glory to God—to lift him up."

"I would say you succeeded, brother," I replied.

Who is John Michael Talbot? Many have followed the young singer's career for well over a decade. To some, he was the young banjo player at an Indiana state fair; to others a balladeer singing songs of love. For an entire generation of early-seventies dropouts, radicals, and students, John sang mellow songs of protest and idealism, dreaming of alternatives for a better world. To the youthful evangelical Christians of the Jesus movement, John was a reformed recording star who had chosen the straight and narrow, gently rocking their souls with contemporary Christian musical messages. Finally, there is a rapidly expanding group for whom John is a Catholic minstrel, softly singing of the ancient apostolic faith, beckoning those who have ears to hear to return to the roots of their spiritual heritage.

There are almost as many different images of John Talbot as there are listeners of his music. Some have wondered which of John's many diverse expressions is the real one. The answer can only be, all of them—all of them in the sense that we all are who we are today because of where we have been yesterday. John is no exception to this rule. His life has been a process and a pilgrimage, an intriguing personal journey evolving toward an increasingly powerful statement of the Gospel of Christ.

In an era of heightened interest in our cultural and spiritual roots, John's prophetic, lyrical call to orthodoxy and liturgical worship are on the cutting edge of today's renewal movement. Certainly there are those who see this young man as a throwback to medievalism—an anachronism robed in sackcloth. There are others, however, who see him as a sign of things to come—the beginning of a powerful new lay movement in the church, and perhaps even in society at large.

In this book we will look at the life of a musician who at the age of fourteen was already touring America, and now, nearly a decade and a half later, is commanding sold-out concerts and huge record sales with his stunningly simple expression of Franciscan spirituality. This book is not a biography as much as it is an unfinished narrative about a troubadour—a troubadour working tirelessly in the service of the Lord.

Where did it start? What were the beginnings of this journey and this dream? In any attempt to observe the life flow of a particular person it is essential to focus on the historical background of the individual in question.

John's mother is Jimmie Margaret Talbot, now a widow living quietly in a modest Indianapolis apartment. Her earliest recollections are of her father, the Reverend James Cochran, an itinerant singing Methodist minister who covered a lot of ground preaching in his home state of Oklahoma. Most of the men in the family were traveling preachers, including Jimmie's grandfather, seven uncles, and brothers.

For much of her life, Jimmie endured nagging illness. During one of her childhood attacks, a woman neighbor made an urgent house call. Not only did she have words of comfort, encouragement, and prayer, but she baptized the Methodist minister's child on the spot. The neighbor, it turned out, was a Catholic.

At the time this curious event left no discernible impression on the little Jimmie, although she did recover fully from her illness. It was only much later that the real significance of this sacramental encounter became evident, and ultimately led her on a path that was to change her life forever.

While the devotion of Jimmie's father to his calling was apparent, there were nonetheless elements of her life as a "preacher's kid" (such as the political machinations of behind-the-scenes church life) that were to produce in later years a kind of spiritual estrangement from her Christian upbringing. But, as is so often the case with prodigals, the eventual homecoming was worth the time of spiritual drift and disillusionment.

Jimmie married Dick Talbot, a good-natured man with a keen sense of humor. Dick bubbled with enthusiasm and was more than just a little strong-willed.

"Dad was an air-force man in World War II," John recalls. "He was based in India and flew those big B-24 bombers over 'the hump' into Burma. Actually, he started out as a pilot but he was booted out of pilot training school because he was always skipping out to see my mother. They dropped him into navigation school where he was promptly bounced because he persisted in his unauthorized visits to Mom. Next came bombardier training where, you guessed it, he was fingered again, after a military policeman discovered him hiding in the trunk of a buddy's car, headed out to see Mom. His romantic inclinations ultimately got him stuck in the dreaded position of tail gunner, where it was all but impossible to bail out in an emergency. As I think back now, I can still remember Dad gazing skyward more than once, recalling the friends he lost during that long, awful war. He was very fortunate to get through it."

Together, Dick and Jimmie established their home, first in Kansas City, Missouri, later in Oklahoma City. The first child was Terry; a year later, Tanni came, followed five years after, in Oklahoma City, by John Michael, born May 8, 1954. All three children inherited their grandfather's gift of song, so it came as no surprise to their parents when the precocious youngsters picked up musical instruments at very early ages.

Their father's job eventually took the family to Little Rock, Arkansas, where John's considerable musical gifts continued to develop, along with athletic ability as a baseball player. In the midst of his youthful pursuits, John remembers many inspiring moments with his father. "I have very, very pleasant memories of Dad. We'd be looking up at the stars—a father and a son, you know, just talking about bigness. 'Dad, do you believe in God?' I asked. 'Oh yeah,' he answered casually. 'Who is he? I wondered. 'Well, Son, he's big—*real* big!'"

John continued, "I recall as a six-year-old having a very special relationship with that big God. One day I was out in the driveway just tossing pebbles into a puddle. I remember clear as day how the Lord created the impression in me that I would either become a doctor or a minister—I wanted to help people to know this goodness that I was then experiencing. But since the sight of blood has always made me sick, I guess that left me with only one option!" John smiled wistfully as he related the incident.

The young man inherited more than the treasure of his grandfather's musical talent. He also received a special grace—the deep inner desire to serve God totally and to seek a vocation appropriate for the task. There were, however, a few unforeseen stops along the way for the youthful pilgrim.

Chapter Two

Seeds of Faith and the Sounds Unlimited

When John was only seven years old, the Talbot family moved from Oklahoma City to Little Rock, Arkansas. This transplant, which was difficult for the entire family, proved even more disturbing to young John, who had come to love their home on Oklahoma City's Pembroke Drive, a place he still remembers as an enchanted chapter in his childhood. And just when Little Rock had begun to feel like home, the family was suddenly uprooted again, when Dick was transferred to Indianapolis in January 1963. Both Jimmie and John remember this particular move as the most stressful of all because, compared to the informality and warmth of the American South, the people of Indiana seemed cold and distant.

Though not inordinately traumatic by the standards of today's transient life-styles, this sense of geographical alienation nevertheless had long-range impact. The family leaned toward a more insular social posture. They stuck to themselves, becoming one another's best friends.

The tight family life experienced by the Talbots was not merely a negative reaction to relocating the household. It was also a fortuitous step toward an uncommon nurturing process that helped to foster the talents and personalities of the individual members—particularly in the areas of creative imagination and music. "We found it nearly impossible to make friends in Indianapolis," John's mother remembers. "I have no doubt that this problem contributed greatly to the children's involvement in music—they missed the popularity they had enjoyed in the other two cities." Spurred by their desire to break the local ice, they plunged into the music world under big brother Terry's leadership and found themselves increasingly well-known and well-received around the neighborhood and at school functions.

Of course, Terry, Tanni, and Johnny played games together around the house, like all other children—well, maybe not *exactly* like other children. As a matter of fact, the Talbot kids were well-known among their peers for their highly imaginative recreational endeavors. Cowboys, Indians, and the world of childhood make-believe are one thing, but real neighborhood theater, complete with props and custom-designed wardrobes, is quite another altogether. The children of the area, and occasionally their parents, were held spellbound for hours as the three aspiring actors performed well-rehearsed little skits and dramas based on popular televison shows or widely read children's stories.

"Mom made it a point to be right in the middle of our make-believe world with us," John remembers. "She would spend days conceiving, designing, and sewing fantastic costumes for our little plays—'Peter Pan,' 'Tarzan,' 'Vikings,' 'Superman.' We left no stone unturned in our attempts at dramatic realism." Later, young John became intensely interested in the history of the American West. In character with their zealous approach to hobbies, John and Terry researched, then painstakingly designed and constructed, a huge balsa wood scale model of the Texas Alamo. "It must have been four feet by four feet!" John chuckles. "I guess you could say we were pretty intense."

Of the three children, John was by far the most keenly expressive of his creative imagination. For him the world of normal youthful make-believe merged with reality—it was occasionally difficult for him to distinguish objective facts from the fiction of theater.

"I really think this was the earliest sign to us of Johnny's deep faith—that he believed so totally," says his mother. "One day Terry and Tanni built a wall of cardboard boxes around John and told him he was in prison. He actually believed he was hopelessly confined—I arrived in his room to find him crying, paralyzed by his absolute certainty that those boxes were as real and solid as any brick jailhouse wall!" It took some coaxing and more than just a little motherly persuasion to get Johnny out of his prison.

John trusted so completely in the myths surrounding Christmas that he refused to accept Santa Claus as merely make-believe. When a classmate ridiculed him for continuing to regard Santa as a real person, his parents decided that perhaps it was time to tell him the truth. At first, John was adamantly opposed to giving up a cherished dream, but eventually he acquiesced with genuine grief. "We really had to be careful with Johnny, because while we didn't want people to laugh at him, we also had to be sensitive about how we broke the spell of childhood fantasies," Tanni reports.

When John was not role playing or toying with his first musical instrument, a drum set, he spent much of his time alone. From the beginning it appears as though John sought out quiet places and natural settings just to sit and think. Nature in itself was a constant source of simple joy to him. He ponders one of those moments, recalling, "I just immensely enjoyed trees, creeks, fields, and living things. One afternoon I overheard my church's retreat director whisper quietly to Mom, 'I find John Michael a very interesting boy—he is totally content just watching the waves on the lake for hours and hours.' And I remember our annual family vacation to Lake Gibson, in Oklahoma. I would go down to the beach, stare at the shimmering ripples of water, and feel at one with nature—awed by it, entranced by it, and I think in a very real sense learning a lot from it. I would creatively visualize, imagine, and just think. It gave me a wonderful warm feeling inside."

Even as a grade-school youth John's love of nature prompted unsettlingly pointed and mature thoughts, preserved in the painstaking scrawl of a particularly insightful elementary-school essay:

THE FOREST

The forest is a green carpet of life spread over the layer of death called earth, which all living creatures return to after dying. In it there are creatures of all shapes and forms. There are running rivers of cool, clear water which bring life into the forest. It can also take life away by the warm, black chemicals of all kinds which destroy the life in the forest and turn the green into a deep, deadly red. The life in the forest reminds us there is still hope of having a peaceful world. Soon there will be no forest in the world and all there will be is hate and the red layer of death we call earth.

There were times when John's love of solitude, nature, and exploration led to brief episodes of family panic: for example, the young naturalist's spontaneous little outing into the woods near his home at age four. Happening upon a moss-covered "fort" undoubtedly constructed years before by other children, John settled in for a few hours of reflection and fantasy while his family anxiously combed the neighborhood for signs of the wayward waif. He would never forget his first "hermitage in the woods" experience—a dream-fantasy that would one day blossom into fulfillment beyond his wildest hopes.

At this juncture in John's biography it should be pointed out that it would be unfair to think of little John Talbot as an introvert or as socially maladjusted. His natural leanings were simply toward quietness and occasional solitude. In many other ways he was a typical rough-and-tumble schoolboy. When it came to baseball, for example, he was the all-American red-blooded kid, with mitt, bat, knees torn out of his pants, and more than his share of innate athletic ability. It was to be the only thing in his growing years that would rival the world of make-believe, and the world of music, which was destined to become his life's primary vocation.

Music was a central feature of Talbot family life, one of those avocations around which they wove much of the fabric of their lives together. Dick played the violin in the Oklahoma Symphony Orchestra, Jimmie could frequently be found at the piano, and the three children would eventually pick up a score of instruments, ranging from tambourine to cello.

John remembers beginning piano lessons when he was six, eventually dropping out, but maintaining his musical interests in general. "There was, shall we say, a not quite active but not really passive drive toward music—it was just part of our family life—it was simply *there*," John recalls.

But things began to change when older brother Terry picked up the guitar one day at age eleven. A casual family pastime suddenly became, for the Talbot children, an alluring pursuit full of fun and possibilities.

Tanni recognized John's awesome musical talent while they were still young children. "I always knew there was something special about him—Johnny was, and is, a true musical genius. Everyone around him could see it. He was given a special gift—I believe it even more today than I did back then."

"It wasn't long before Terry decided he wanted to start a band," John recalls. "He brought some school friends over to the house to play music and sing. I was about seven, I guess, and I just listened, wishing I could be a part of it all. I knew I wanted to sing, and when I actually tried, it felt incredibly rewarding, like I was giving expression for the first time to something deep inside."

But John's enthusiasm was dampened by an unusual problem: he could hear harmonies perfectly but had serious trouble with melodies.

One day after school John came home and sheepishly announced to his mother that he had been flunked by his music teacher. "What?" she exclaimed incredulously. "You, Johnny? That's impossible!" She marched to the school with her son firmly in tow and politely requested a meeting with the teacher. "Mr. Wallis, I know Johnny can sing. He can sing better than any child his age I've ever heard, in fact. But sometimes, well, he gets a little nervous. And another thing you should know—he only sings harmonies." A second chance for John demonstrated to his teacher that while the youngster faltered slightly in melody parts he was brilliant in picking out and singing harmonies, especially in high ranges. The point was made and John received an A in his music class that semester.

His confidence restored and enthusiasm ignited, John listened with intent razor-sharp ears as Terry and his friends honed their skills singing folk songs in the family living room. When the fledgling group encountered vocal complications, Terry would ask John to arrange the parts in question. This, coupled with his ability to hit what for others were impossibly high notes, gave him an increased sense of belonging to the group. "I could actually hit a high D or high E with no problem whatever. Most high tenors do well to reach B-flat. Now with potential like that, Terry began to invite me to participate, in spite of the age difference between us. At nine I was close to being accepted as a member of what we were loosely coming to regard as a band."

The musical instruments that John eventually mastered include guitar, banjo, dobro, pedal steel, bass—the list goes on, but he will always recall with special fondness that first drum. "Dad gave it to me as a gift and of course I played around with it pretty regularly for awhile. Then one day I watched in utter amazement as a guy on TV played a banjo—I was totally captivated. Immediately I ran to my room and began attempting to transform my drum head into a banjo. Dad gave me a banjo and I eventually took lessons from Steve Lawrence, who had studied under Jerry Waller, who at that time was considered the best banjo player in those parts."

Ultimately, John built a solid reputation as one of the best banjo players in the area. He played classical banjo as well as popular music. Tanni remembers John's only significant impediment in furthering his ability on the banjo: "Johnny taught himself, for the most part, which we all found amazing. While the rest of us worked hard to master an instrument, Johnny would just pick one up and feel his way through it with that special gift of his. He could play anything he set his mind to. When it came to banjo, nobody could teach him for very long because he could pick it up so readily. It wouldn't be long before he was actually teaching new things to his banjo teachers! 'There's nothing more I can do with this kid,' they would say."

Meanwhile Terry was fully determined to have a successful musical group. A natural leader and highly charismatic individual, Terry recruited three talented friends from the school choir into a musical combination that also included his sister. They called themselves the Quinn Chords. John's big moment came late one afternoon as he and Terry sat in their bedroom talking things over. "John, you know we need a good high tenor in the group. We need a change. Would you like to help us out?"

Incredulous, John responded cautiously, "Sure Terry, you know I'll continue to help you pick your parts and harmonies."

"I'm not talking *help*, John. I want you *in*. As a full member of the Quinn Chords." John's heart skipped a beat but he concealed his joy with a tentative grin. Terry, Tanni, and John were now full partners in their budding musical enterprise.

A few weeks later the band entered the "Hoosier Hootenanny" at the Indiana State Fair, urged on by friends who had heard their practice sessions. To their surprise and elation, they placed second in the competition. The Quinn Chords soon began to receive requests to appear at shopping centers, bank openings, and department stores. John still remembers their first professional engagement: "I'll admit, I was scared to death. There's no way around it. I couldn't bear to look straight at the people in the audience, so the whole time we were up there I stared at the microphone directly in front of my face as we played and sang. Afterward, Mom came up to me and said, 'You sounded wonderful, John, but cross-eyed tenors just don't make it, honey. Smile at the people.'"

Inspired by such contemporary folk artists as Peter, Paul, and Mary; the Chad Mitchell Trio; and the New Christy Minstrels; the Quinn Chords knuckled down to serious practice sessions. John, while finding music fun and expressive, soon discovered that success does not come without a good many hours of hard labor, endless practice, calloused fingers, and late nights. Raw talent in itself is simply not enough. By twelve he was relentlessly pushing for perfection. "Mom and Dad were a big help. They were always so supportive and encouraging when it came to our music. They never pushed us; they were simply there, available, coaching, assisting, wanting the very best for us. They were both Depression-era kids, you know, and they were just tickled that we could pursue an area of interest that they couldn't have dreamed of when they were kids. In fact, it is undoubtedly because of their own austere upbringing that they were committed to the idea that we should have the opportunity to experience music."

In September 1967, Terry and John entered their group, now called the Four Score, in a "battle of the bands" contest at the Indianapolis Young America Fair. They not only won the much publicized championship but landed a recording contract as well, punching out a crisp little single entitled "Little Brother," which was aired on local radio. Although the influence of the Byrds and the Hollies, two internationally famous groups of the day, is apparent on the cut, a specific and unique Talbot-brothers style had already begun to emerge. It wasn't really rock 'n' roll, western, or purely folk—it was an elusive, appealing blend, a distinctive sound that would evolve throughout their career.

An interesting stylistic development was the group's brief excursion into psychedelic-acid rock when they feared that folk music, their forte, was on the decline. After listening to one of their tapes, a friend in the music business challenged them bluntly: "This stuff is garbage. This isn't *you!* Get back to your folk roots, boys. You've gotta be true to your real musical identities!" They took his advice. Without a second look at trendy musical fads, they pressed on with their folk-rock style and vowed to be artistically true to themselves.

Four Score turned out to be a short-lived transitional bridge between the Quinn Chords and what was to become an even more successful group, the Sounds Unlimited, which featured John squarely in the middle of an extremely promising combo as rhythm guitarist and vocalist. And all at the tender age of twelve.

"That was a real turning point," John recalls with a touch of nostalgia. "We became more professional— Terry especially became educated to the possibilities of being a top regional rock 'n' roll band. We began to tour the local area and drew surprisingly large crowds, mostly working weekends at high-school proms, parties, things like that." In the meantime, Tanni was forced to drop out of the band because of illness, but she continued to follow the progress of her brothers with great interest.

John and Terry ate, drank, and slept music, building a brotherly alliance that would blend more than just their complementary voices—they pooled their growing musical talents and business sense into a well-oiled little machine that landed the Sounds in dozens of newspaper columns, radio shows, and magazine articles. In March 1967, *Teen Tempo* magazine featured the brothers and their band in a five-page photo spread, heaping praise on the young Talbots:

> Terry . . . is one of the most respected young guitarists in the state. You can see he is a real showman . . . , keeping a fast, steady pace a teen crowd likes.
>
> The fourth member of the group, John Talbot, is perhaps the most surprising. John, who at twelve is the youngest member of any Indianapolis rock group, doesn't let his age get in the way. In fact, John seems to be the one who

commands your attention most during a performance. He has his own musical opinions which he lets others know about. He says, "I wish we could do music we like and not worry about the crowd."

Obviously, John had begun to show his independent colors a bit—a hint of the proverbial "temperamental artist." The Sounds Unlimited met in the Talbot home for frequent practice sessions, listening to the records of the Beatles, Judy Collins, Joan Baez, and the Byrds until they felt they had captured every lick and lyric to absolute perfection.

When asked how his overall childhood was affected by youthful showbiz pursuits, John responds philosophically, "I was in a professional environment from the time I was nine or ten years old; of course, there are liabilities. For example, occasional sibling conflicts were often left dangling until after a performance. You know, the show must go on! So in that respect, professional considerations sometimes eclipsed personal needs, but never to the point of real crisis. On the positive side, I would have to say that it gave us a real sense that there were things much bigger than our own petty problems—ideas worth sacrificing for, I suppose you could say." He goes on to point out another advantage of life in a band. "I've always said my road experiences, even at age twelve, prepared me for the rigors of life in a Christian community. We had to travel, eat, sleep, and perform together and make it work—we learned collaboration and mutual respect in very tight quarters at pretty early ages."

When I realized how much time these kids had been sinking into their new venture, I had to ask how this had affected their schooling—how did they balance the Sounds with their school obligations? "Well, needless to say that was quite a challenge," says John, who has an IQ above 150. "I was consistently in the upper level of my class, although I must confess that professionally related absences made things rather tough on us at times. Our parents promised the school authorities that we would be kept current on all subjects, to which the teachers responded with, shall we say, guarded co-operation. I don't think we ever let them down. And our classmates were highly supportive. They saw us as being on the cutting edge of the youth culture and were fascinated."

The one area where the teachers and the Talbots clashed was, certainly by today's standards, somewhat trivial: hair length. Both John and Terry wore their hair long enough to cover the top of their ears and brush their collar. In the eyes of the school principal, this was scandalous. "We had come to associate long hair with more than stage presence," argues John. "We began to associate long hair with people who were making statements of social relevance in a very troubled world and we were serious about moving in the same direction ourselves. It was a visual image we felt we needed to be identified with. The school authorities fought us every step of the way. When you stop and think about it, both sides wasted a lot of time acting and reacting on this issue, but it was important to us then, of course."

As for spiritual things, John summarized his earliest recollections of church in just two words: "incredibly boring." While he loved thinking about God and was intrigued with this mystical prophet named Jesus, his view of established Christianity tended toward the negative. It just didn't seem to match his own intuitive notions of religious ideals. God somehow seemed to speak more clearly, more perceptibly, to him through nature. He saw trees, in particular, as symbols of deeply rooted, changeless absolutes in a fast-paced, transitory world. They whispered to him in the breeze; it was God's language.

As the late sixties exploded upon America with the winds of change and social upheaval, the Talbot brothers prepared themselves for what they knew deep within would be a boisterous ride to professional success. They had drive, talent, and a gift for being in the right place at the right time. As if they had been born to it, success was not a matter of *if*, but *when*.

Young John Michael Talbot was now well into his personal script, that is, he was participating in a life process whereby patterns of behavior tend to perpetuate themselves within a family from one generation to the next. Psychiatrist Eric Berne called this behavioral-selection phenomenon "scripting,"[1] and defined it as a life plan based on decisions made in childhood, reinforced by parents, justified by subsequent events, and culminating in a chosen alternative. Born into a musical family of itinerant ministers, John had already begun to play, sing, travel, and communicate a message from his own soul to a waiting world.

However, lest we see the young man as a merely predictable link in a sequence of family characteristics, it must be said that John possessed his own unique inner direction. He was a loner, a thinker, and an innovator. Herein lies the key to his peerless journey.

Chapter Three

Mason Proffit—
A Brand New Sound

The Talbot brothers' rise to musical fame was not meteoric, not the proverbial rags-to-riches leap into stardom, but a more process-oriented progression of planning, timing, luck—and work.

The Sounds Unlimited continued to pull themselves together through more rehearsals, performances, and tedious hours of practice that would frequently sail off into jam sessions which allowed spontaneity and unbridled musical enthusiasm to burst forth in crescendos of wild sound. After one such evening at the Talbot home in Indianapolis, the ad-lib guitar and banjo riffs trailed off as the four tired musicians prepared to call it quits for the evening. They were preparing for an engagement at a Chicago hangout called the Cellar. It was early in the summer of 1968.

"Hey, guys, we are on to something." Terry leaned over his electric guitar with an unmistakable look of ambition in his eyes. "I really think we can make it happen—recording and touring—I mean hittin' the whole damn country, not just local stuff." His voice, hoarse from practice, was calm and deliberate, but the edge of elation at the prospect of hitting the jackpot was definitely present as he spoke. And the elation was catching.

The contagion rocketed John to his feet. "You know, we really need to sit down with Bill and do some serious planning—he was right about our folk roots, wasn't he?"

Indeed, record producer Bill Trout seemed the right person to assist the fledgling group into the world of professional entertainment on the national level. It was he who had confronted the Sounds in their experimentation with psychedelic rock, urging them to reexamine their musical style. Thus far, his advice had proven right. When the Sounds hit Chicago's Cellar with a revised lineup of folk-rock tunes, the place went mad with uproarious cheering. It was time, Terry thought, to sit down with Trout, who had produced their singles, "Little Brother" and "A Girl As Sweet As You."

After a long meeting, Bill summed up his thinking. "You guys have real potential, there's no doubt about that. Go heavier on the folk, lighter on the rock 'n' roll, and dump the psychedelic stuff. John, you're one of the best banjo pickers in the Midwest, and Terry, you have what it takes as a folk guitarist. Why don't you load up that folk sound with bass and drums and see what comes out?"

"Okay, Bill," Terry answered. "We're tired of small time. We want to make it big, you know. We want to go national."

"Then go out and do it! You guys are real good. And another thing, you boys ought to start writing some of your own songs."

The Sounds Unlimited opened their throttles. They scheduled more practice sessions, continued local gigs, and pursued individual expertise, energizing their efforts by dreaming of what might be happening to them. They decided that perhaps a new name for the group was in order.

"We felt it was important to have a new 'handle' for the group," John remembers. "We went home, put our brains to it and came up with a name based on Credence Clearwater Revival's first record, calling ourselves the Mason Proffit Reunion, later shortening it to Mason Proffit. We liked the name Proffit because Frank Proffit wrote the song "Tom Dooley." We chose Mason because it had a kind of gutsy folk feel about it—maybe there was a subconscious tie with mason jars—I don't know."

Terry then insisted that a recognizable visual image was necessary to package the group. They looked to other groups who served as inspiration. The Byrds had become a bit too slick, too polished in appearance, and the Flying Burrito Brothers, well, they had turned to flashy custom-tailored cowboy suits. Ultimately, they settled on an American woodsman look, complete with leathers, buckskins, and hats, giving them the appearance of a ragged band of buffalo hunters. They let their beards grow and their hair flowed like General Custer's.

Mason Proffit showed up at events previously scheduled for the Sounds Unlimited. They were an immediate hit with the crowd. Everywhere they went there were invitations to return.

"Yes, we were hungry for success and all that goes along with it, but for Terry and me there was more to it," says John. "What so impressed us about Peter, Paul, and Mary, Joan Baez, and other popular folk artists were their strong messages. Sure, the music in itself was impressive, without question, but it was the fabulous integration of music with social comment that reached Terry and me. These people communicated from their hearts, from the deepest levels of their souls, about things that affected the real world."

"You mean, things like Vietnam?" I asked.

"Exactly. Vietnam, the draft, war, racial issues, and injustice in general. We wanted hits but we also wanted meaning and relevance."

So the Talbot brothers and their growing entourage packed their instruments and buckskins from town to town, captivating audiences who identified with their plaintive cries for equality, justice, and brotherly love. They became tunesmiths, crafting parables and rhymes wrapped in foot-stomping rhythms. John and Terry collaborated on the songwriting. John specialized in the music while Terry's strength was in writing lyrics. They became an unbeatable team. Their creativity seemed to blend as compatibly as their voices.

A number of adjustments were made as the band's reputation grew. The banjo and guitar, while providing a country feel, did not carry the soul of the sound they really sought. It was decided someone should play a pedal-steel guitar. A flip of the coin landed John in that role—another expansion on his seemingly endless musical talent.

"I just went down to Arthur's Music Store in Indianapolis, picked up a pedal steel and learned to play it in about three weeks. I listened to every pedal-steel record I could lay my hands on and plunged in—I wasn't highly skilled but good enough to get by," John recalls with characteristic modesty.

The band, now consisting of five members (John, Terry, Tim Ayres, Arty Nash, and Ron Schueter) were playing to packed houses and standing ovations by 1969. They continued to develop their sound with a special emphasis on a very tight three-part harmony, unusual for pop musicians of that time. They adapted folk music to rock and social commentary to create what John called "a kind of social comment, folk-country rock group," indicating the problem people would aways encounter in trying to define their music. As soon as a local reviewer would label them folk, they moved toward country. Then the heavy percussion seemed to give them more of a rock 'n' roll feel. Their eclectic approach made them tantalizingly elusive to those seeking to pin them down with stereotypical adjectives. They were simply Mason Proffit, that exciting new band with a novel sound.

The stimulation of the enthusiastic audiences and the exhilaration of success seemed to embolden the lads, especially Terry. The cause-oriented musical format became a soapbox from which he began sharing his ideas with the crowd. "He started to speak out a little between songs. We would be playing—jamming, you know, just winging it like a jazz combo—and suddenly Terry would stop and get up to the mike and start preaching while the band boogied in the background! He'd say something about Vietnam and the throng would wind up into an absolute fervor—it was awesome," John remembers, recalling images of Terry strutting on stage. "When Terry grew his hair and mustache and put on that broad-brimmed hat, something happened. It didn't happen with any of the rest of us, but it happened with Terry. To this day, if he grows that big mustache and puts on a hat, there's a vibe about it. It's really amazing."

John relates an incident from an Ohio concert a year or two later. "Terry, with his special gift to enthrall crowds, is whipping up an audience. This makes the local cops really nervous. They step up to Terry and suggest that maybe he could help keep the lid on. Terry knows the police and the owner of the building are apprehensive so he has a little fun when the stage lighting proved somewhat inadequate. He stops the music, steps up to the microphone and, with all these screaming people in the palm of his hand, shouts, 'Hey, you folks. If I ask you to shoot the lights out of this place, would you do it?' 'Yeaaaaa . . .' comes a unified, moblike response. Terry finds himself, shall we say, politely ushered out of the hall by the sheriff. When it came to audiences, Terry really had it. Still does." There is a hint of brotherly admiration in John's narration.

The band's initial invigoration quickly turned into a cool-headed approach to career development. The next move was into the recording studio. They put a record out by releasing what they had intended as a demo tape. Once again, Bill Trout helped. "This is sounding pretty good, boys. Why don't we go with it. Let's sell records to anyone who'll buy them." It seemed like a rather freewheeling approach, but it worked.

In the beginning, John recalls, studio sessions were fast, the music tight and well-rehearsed. There was a very disciplined approach to getting into the studio, recording, and getting out, which saved both production money and everyone's nerves. Their first album was a product of Chicago's Universal Studios; later they switched to Paragon Recording Studios.

In the simpler days of recording technology, vocals were done with the three singers clustered around a single mike. John's high-tenor parts forced him to sing so loudly that the others made him back up until he was all the way across the room. This created a few laughs in the midst of the pressures and stress of tedious hours in soundproof booths.

With the release of their first album, *Two Hangmen*, the Mason Proffit band hit the road running. They encountered nothing but wild acclaim everywhere they performed, much to the annoyance of some other bands. "A problem began to develop with the more established bands we toured with," observes John. "We played with the greats of that era—Iron Butterfly, Arlo Guthrie, Janis Joplin, the Flying Burrito Brothers, Canned Heat. We appeared with the Nitty Gritty Dirt Band, the Grateful Dead, Jefferson Airplane—I can't remember them all now. I do remember a young blond entertainer who opened for us when he was still on the college circuit—John Denver. The problem was simply that we often upstaged the top billing. With us, crowds went berserk. They would scream, clap, yell, and tear up seats when we performed, and then level out when the main act appeared."

A graphic case in point was their first big tour, which took them to Seattle, Spokane, Yakima, Vancouver, B.C., and Portland with the then popular group, the Youngbloods, who established themselves in rock history with their hit single "Get Together." Halfway through the tour trouble boiled over behind the scenes because of the crowd's different reactions to the two groups. "We came on stage at full tilt, flat out, going for broke—we had those audiences dancing, clapping, and singing with us, which was very unusual at the time. We got them up, but when the Youngbloods came out, they put the crowd into a pot-smoking lull. Their music was technically very good—beautiful sounds—but they just mellowed the crowd, while we stoked them, and that created a bit of friction for awhile."

Northwest disc jockey Ichabod Caine recalls that first tour through the state of Washington: "I'll always remember that occasion because the Youngbloods were so hot at the time—really in demand—and along comes this new band opening for them, Mason Proffit. They were incredibly tight as a group; their music was fantastic. I remember later playing a number of their tunes on the air. 'Two Hangmen' was especially good." Caine, now at Seattle's KPLZ radio station, kept his eye on the Talbots. "It's incredibly interesting to see where these guys have gone, how they have developed as artists and as people with real purpose in their lives."

And the fans, the loyal followers, were another dimension to the story. From the beginning Mason Proffit had a nationwide following, some of whom still collect old albums with the zeal of antique dealers. Many were young women looking for a shot at the rising young rockers, joining other hapless groupies and hangers-on around the buses, vans, dressing rooms, and hotel lobbies. What promising youth on his way to stardom wouldn't be enthused at the prospect of beautiful girls seeking somehow to validate themselves by bedding down with a rock star? It had to happen—innocence faded, and as the mystique of Mason Proffit grew, doubt and philosophical questioning filled the mind of sixteen-year-old John: What about that childhood God, so big and so special?

In the face of a quickening professional pace and an accelerating touring schedule, Terry and John now feel they lost their way spiritually. To fill the void, they clung even more tightly to the causes celebrated in their music, pumping out their message with near evangelistic zeal. They were now at the very center of a questioning counterculture—they were among its elite spokesmen. As John says, he had become "a revolutionary, lyrically prophetic, free-living folk-rocker."

Inevitably, life on the road lost its glamour after a few thousand miles. Cars, buses, planes, airports, and hotel rooms now blur together in John's mind. "We would get up at five or six in the morning after having been up until two or three, pack our gear, check in at the airport, fly, load luggage, take another bus to a hotel, grab a quick meal, do a gig at a college or auditorium, get to our hotel around two or three in the morning, try to eat, sleep an hour or two, and do it all over again the next day. I don't care who you are, that gets old."

A life of frenzied intercity touring was interrupted only long enough for more recording sessions. John and Terry seemed like bottomless wells brimming with creative songwriting and arrangements. FM radio stations took the lead in airing their music, while albums rolled off the presses by the hundreds of thousands. *Two Hangmen* was followed by *Moving toward Happiness, Last Night I Had the Strangest Dream, Rockfish Crossing, Bareback Rider,* and *Come and Gone.* Once the records began moving briskly, Warner Brothers signed a contract with them. Each album showed marked improvement musically and technically over the previous release.

Mason Proffit was on a "roll," heading for the top, riding the wave of revolutionary fervor that almost tore the nation in two during the troubled late sixties and early seventies. The Talbot brothers were pioneering a new sound that would later come to be known as country rock, a sound that would one day make groups like the Eagles enormously rich and famous.

Many of the band's album cuts were radio favorites, and Mason Proffit's fans will immediately recall such hits as "Freedom," "500 Men," "Eugene Pratt," "Buffalo," "Jesse," and the chartbusters, "Two Hangmen" and "A Thousand and Two." It's not unusual in some regions to hear some of these tunes still on the air today.

It is interesting to look back on the lyrics of certain songs for historical perspective. The *cause* remains uncompromised throughout the Mason Proffit era, with special emphases on the oppressed and downtrodden. Soldiers, American Indians, migrant workers, truckdrivers, and lovers are championed in turn.

Of particular interest are lyrics that seem to foreshadow John and Terry's spiritual paths:

500 MEN

500 came,
500 died,
I can still see them burning.
The bodies of the young,

the bodies of the old,
for the times were returning.
For on Texas ground we lie
and dreaming of a heaven,
not one man hates,
not one man cries,
if we could only take a learning.
From the stories I'm told, men die for their
    right
to live in nature's freedom,
they fought by day, and loved by the night
where only God could see them.
But today a multitude
of men, of love, are dying
and killing in the name of peace
and listening to nature's crying.
And we call for you Mary, the mother of our
    Savior,
and we cry for you Jesus, the minister of love,
and we pray for the people, helping other peo-
    ple—
their time's going to come.
Today in 1971
God's children are not fighting.
But the devil still, he finds his ways
to the hearts that heed a guiding.
So today the evil in man
is sparking self-destruction
from the fires that they loot and choke
the breath of life—
if we could only turn to loving,
if we could only turn to loving,
if we could only turn to loving,
if we could only turn to loving. . . .[1]

WERE YOU THERE?

You said something should be done—
the way your slaves were shot and hung.
You said all men should be free—

were you there at Wounded Knee?
Were you living in '42?
You cried when Hitler killed the Jews,
you said that no race should have to die—
were you there at My Lai?
Were you there when they called my country down,
did you see her when she finally hit the ground,
could you feel the tears she shed,
were you there when Jesus bled?
Come all ye youth, it's time
to take a stand,
You have salvation in your hand,
we need your words and, lo,
we need your minds,
we need you straight, not stoned and blind.
Were you there when we walked across the land,
was that you with a rifle in your hand?
Don't try to run, don't try to hide,
were you there when freedom died? . . .[2]

BETTER FIND JESUS

Talkin' about the world
and how it's wrong and right,
you're screaming for peace
and then you're ready to fight,
Throwing a brick in the name of love—
Talkin', but you never settle anything.
refrain: You'd better find Jesus,
     you'd better find Jesus,
     you'd better find Jesus,
     you'd better find love.

Let's take a look now at My Lai,
Listen to a soldier, listen to his side.
He'll tell you about an old woman,
she'll come running up to you,
you receive her, she throws you a bomb,
and you're through.
     (refrain)

You may not agree with what I'm trying to
   say—
let me tell you brother, that's okay.
I ain't gonna push on to you
what I believe,
but it might work for you
'cause it works for me.
   (refrain)[3]

In going back over their songs, I am struck by the
soul with which Terry sings, the depth with which John
writes. Their love songs impart a haunting nostalgia, a
"remember when" quality that evokes the listener's personal recollections. "Till the Sun's Gone," a cut from the
album *Come and Gone*, typifies their skillful interplay of
tune and lyric.

Hope is a recurring Talbot theme and seems to un-
derlie their view that some kind of utopia is theoretically
within human reach: "I dreamed the world had all
agreed to put an end to war,/ guns and swords and uni-
forms were scattered on the ground."[4] The lyrics depict
a hopeful dream, yet the soulful tune grieves over the
reality of the hopelessly bellicose state of international
affairs.

The Talbot brothers' songs evoke powerful emotions, from the pain of divorce to the desire to escape
and simply "sail away." Their tunes and lyrics communicate an intense, vulnerable honesty.

National publications and trade journals jumped on
the Mason Proffit story. *Billboard* magazine, the music
industry's bible, touted the group, exclaiming, "This has
to be one of the most exciting groups on the scene."
Seed, a pop-music tabloid, observed, "They've got the
rare ability to grab a crowd's attention . . . and leave
them cheering." One of the nation's largest student
magazines wrote that "Mason Proffit was for a time
[nearly two years] one of the top ten paid groups in the
country, making eight to ten thousand dollars a night.
In some cities they drew as many as nineteen thousand
people."

On occasion, the Talbots went back home to visit their family. It seemed as though they were getting all they could handle in the way of publicity, money, recording opportunities, and concerts—with more of the same coming down the line. John and Terry looked forward to brief respites—quiet moments with Mom, Dad, and Tanni, away from record executives, accountants, public-relations people, agents, managers, and the omnipresent entourage of those seeking a slice of a rapidly growing financial pie.

"Are you boys taking good care of yourselves?" Jimmie frequently asked.

"Yeah, Mom, we're doing great," came the standard reply.

By this time the band had moved to Encino, California, a twenty-minute drive from Hollywood. As with so many others, the promise of fame and fortune lured them to the coast of southern California, where thousands of would-be entertainers live out their fantasies in the fast lane. Jimmie had every right to be worried about her boys. Stories of excessive indulgence and self-destruction in the world of rock 'n' roll were commonplace.

Meanwhile, John and Terry were more than just a little uneasy about their parents' health. Dick had heart trouble and Jimmie remembers health crises which nearly put her out of circulation altogether. "My illnesses began with stomach ailments and many hospital visits. On one occasion I nearly died from a perforated ulcer and later lost eighty-five percent of my stomach and small intestines in an operation. Next I underwent surgery to correct two ruptured disks in my lower back. This trouble continued for several years, during which time I was heavily sedated. Naturally, my memory of this time is clouded—those were the years that Mason Proffit was taking off and recording with Warner Brothers." Jimmie adds, "I'm sure my family became more self-reliant because of my illness."

Undoubtedly the Talbot family, especially the boys, were shifting for themselves and doing quite well. However, decreased parental supervision and wide-open living was not without its drawbacks, particularly for sixteen-year-old John, now a seasoned veteran of three bands and years on the rough road of ceaseless professional touring.

"We were still on the upswing," says John. "And things got a little loose all the way around. You've got to remember, Dan, the whole country was in transition socially, morally—even religiously with the new 'Jesus movement' and Eastern cults. Even my parents weren't without their own doubts during this time, and we all felt this kind of 'wait a minute, what's it all about' type of feeling."

John's already philosophically inquisitive mind was filled with questions about God, justice, morality, lifestyle and the quest for absolute meaning in a world of shifting, relativistic thought. He searched for an anchor, a rock, a foundation for life in a heaving sea of change and uncertainty. And in a touring rock band, where personal relationships are frequently temporary and at times stormy, John, on an almost subconscious level, looked for some kind of intimacy, a relationship that would provide love and stability.

He looked much older than his sixteen years, with a full beard, solid build, and eyes that had seen a lot— probably too much. And the company he kept was older—more Terry's age, early twenties. So it came as no surprise when a nineteen-year-old beauty just out of modeling school took a fancy to the young band member. "It was a surprise to me," John says with a faint smile, recalling a handwritten note passed to him through a mutual friend. "It was a brief suggestive message that left no doubt about her intentions, and, I must say, I was quite receptive. I guess that's really where our relationship started." That was back in Chicago during road tours. "As I remember now, it was right as I was beginning to do some serious soul-searching that I met Nancy." John later discovered that the note that launched their relationship was written not by Nancy but by her friend!

Their relationship soon blossomed into a dizzying romance. They seemed perfectly suited in spite of almost three years' difference in age. Nancy began spending a lot of time in the Talbot family home when John was out on the road.

Swept up in the passion of young love and the no-holds-barred atmosphere of an increasingly permissive society, John and Nancy became sexually involved early in their relationship. Making no attempt to cover up, John invited Nancy to live with him in the Mason Proffit "band house" in California. John knew his parents would disapprove. "But what could they do?" he asks. "They were in Indianapolis and we were either in California or on the road. And remember, they were both ill. And Terry, God bless him, tried to watch over me in the way older brothers do, but he didn't really possess a strong moral perspective at that time regarding my situation."

As things turned out, John had underestimated his father, who demanded that Nancy move out of the house. "You are a minor, John, you know that. And she is an adult." Dick's voice crackled over the phone with uncharacteristic anger. "I'll call in the law if I have to."

Shocked, John and Nancy considered their plight and opted for marriage, which they agreed would solve their immediate problem. John's mother recalls her own feelings. "When I learned they were living together I was very distraught. He was only sixteen! I just couldn't accept the situation. When they decided to marry my reaction was 'Hallelujah!' At least they wouldn't be 'living in sin' anymore. Besides, if I had been asked to choose a wife for my son, I probably would have chosen Nancy. She possessed all the attributes of a good wife, and she was beautiful."

In 1971, five months before his eighteenth birthday, John and Nancy were married in an Indianapolis Methodist church. One of John's deep regrets is the total lack of competent premarital counseling he and Nancy received. "Our marital preparation was zip. All we had was our own experience. We went to a pastor one after-

noon and we talked about guitars, you know, and that
was our counseling."

In the early days of the marriage, John and Nancy
experienced the glow and hope of their new start, but it
was to be short-lived. John found that his inner search
for truth had not ended after all; in fact, following the
wedding John felt even more lost, alone, confused. His
inner spiritual journey, in spite of its faltering questions
and doubts, was becoming extremely intense. He began
to withdraw deeper into himself, frequently seeking the
consolation of solitude. Less than a month after their
wedding, Nancy approached John with sad eyes and
more on her mind than she cared to admit—even to herself. "John—we've made a mistake. You should be a
monk." He was stunned but not altogether surprised at
what had become painfully obvious in recent weeks.

A solemn expression sweeps John's countenance as
he relates that pivotal conversation. "Believe it or not,
she said I should become a monk. She wasn't a Catholic,
I wasn't a Catholic, yet she sensed somehow that I was
meant to be a spiritual hermit, a pilgrim moving toward
monasticism. I talked her out of it—persuaded her that
we could make it work. God knows we tried."

Mason Proffit was on top of the world, winning critical recognition for their recordings and nationwide concert tours. If there were personal adversities being
experienced by the boys in the band, they somehow dis-
solved into the background when the buckskinned idols
swaggered on stage to face bright lights and the shrill,
charged cheering of their growing constituency. It was
like a powerful drug, assuaging guilt, fear, and pain,
and drawing them into a hot rush of exuberant musical
abandon. They had become the flagship of a troubled
generation; the soul and conscience of a national counterculture movement. At all costs, the show had to go
on.

Chapter Four

The Rocky Road of Rock 'n' Roll

When one takes a thoughtful look at the pop-music arena, the axiom that immediately comes to mind is, not surprisingly, "What goes up, must come down." In the established annals of rock trivia it is possible to find extremely wide-ranging careers, from the likes of Little Eva, whose hit single, "Locomotion," bought her a one-time tidal wave of attention for a few brief months, all the way to the nearly legendary Rolling Stones, who have survived more than twenty years of tortuous rock 'n' roll living.

On the pop-music scale, Mason Proffit may be found somewhere in the middle, having endured the hungry years of paying their dues while moving toward success, which graced them for about four years. By 1971 they had attracted the eyes and ears of America's most sought-after producers and record companies. Everything about Mason Proffit made them seem ripe for the big time. They were tight and together musically, and ready to face life on the road. They were proven in the recording studio and wrote most of their own material, which was very popular on the concert circuit.

When asked how the band members dealt with one another under the continued stress of demanding road tours, John smiles and relates what seems to typify the occasional stormy moments. "Overall, we got along quite well—we liked each other—but there were times when a disagreement would surface. There would usually be a flash of tempers and a few angry words, followed by business as usual. But there were situations that became rather physical."

John recollects an incident that took place in Racine, Wisconsin. "I'll never forget the time we played one of our first big concerts; four thousand or more people came. Tim and my brother fell into what we thought was a minor altercation during a break between sets. Now, I should explain that Tim had his temper—he was always storming out saying, 'I quit,' but then he would come back later with a cooler head and things would be fine. So as the concert ends, our road manager, Ronnie Sales, is all excited about how well things went and how responsive the crowd was. He was bringing some disc jockeys back to meet us, one of whom was Scotty Brink of WCFL in Chicago, who later became a good friend. By this time we were backstage and Terry and Tim were arguing rather forcefully about something that happened during the show. Ronnie burst into the room and said, 'Hi, guys. I want you to meet Scotty Brink,' at which point Scotty steps into the dressing room as a bass guitar, thrown at Terry by Tim, flies two inches in front of his smiling face."

John laughs and continues. "Anyone who knows the inner workings of a rock band expects those kinds of things to happen, especially in the midst of demanding tour schedules. Later there were more profound differences between us, such as artistic direction, but back then things were rolling along in high gear," he adds. "We seemed to attract attention and terrific crowds."

Then there was the drawing power of the personalities themselves—two good-looking, articulate brothers who seemed to charm the masses with their horseplay one minute and their deeply held social convictions the next. Joe Smith, then president of Warner Brothers, was beginning to feel the excitement of the Mason Proffit magic—they were just about ready, he thought, to step into superstardom. He kept a watchful eye on the group, waiting for the opportune moment to arrive.

Ironically, it was at this very time of the group's professional development that John began to harbor inner questions and doubts about the direction of things, not only relative to the band, but in regard to his own life. His relationship with Nancy was becoming more unsettling with each new suggestion that perhaps their life directions were more divergent than parallel. In John's words, "Nancy was, and is, a beautiful, wonderful person. She was a good wife and a great homemaker—she was, in many ways, what some would call the perfect mate. And I can honestly say that we loved each other." But somehow, young love was just not enough to span the chasm that widened between them and was more ideological and philosophical than physical or emotional. It was difficult to pinpoint the problem. It was simply there, descending like a thickening fog, dampening communication and chilling the atmosphere. Their sheer inability to diagnose specifically the emotional malady they shared created a sense of helplessness and depression—something new for both. But they continued to hang on to hope and to memories of the dream they once held. Perhaps new life could be breathed into the marriage—just maybe there would be a miracle for them.

Beyond his domestic concerns, John attempted to ignore what appeared to be slight inklings of disillusionment with the music industry. "Where is all this going?" he wondered to himself with increasing frequency. "Where does it end?"

He pondered his situation late one evening in early 1971, as the Mason Proffit bus rolled down an interstate freeway toward one more concert in yet another city on a heavily booked tour. The muffled howl of the tires churning against the pavement provided the backdrop to John's meandering thoughts. Terry lay draped across two seats, fast asleep, while the drummer, Arty, stared vacantly out the window, rapping his drumsticks against the seat in front of him. Everyone else, exhausted from weeks of travel, slept soundly.

A swirl of critical issues crowded John's mind. Each seemed to demand his total attention but one stood out from the rest: the revolution everyone was singing and demonstrating about. Mason Proffit, in its touring heyday, was taking its band members through the college campuses and streets of America, where a young generation was calling Uncle Sam on the carpet in a big way. Civil-rights marches and antiwar rallies were seizing the country in convulsions of national conscience. Even upper-middle-class business executives were privately doubting the wisdom of a protracted war halfway around the world that could not be easily explained, even by the Pentagon. As John searched his heart and soul for his role in the protest, he happened upon a very unsettling fact. Those who were shouting down the war in Vietnam were building—and detonating—bombs of their own. Many of those who marched for peace were at war with the system, and were not above using violence in which people were occasionally killed or injured.

"I saw all this as incredibly inconsistent," John remembers now. "These people who were behind much of the antiwar movement were busy assembling their own armies and weapons. The Weather Underground and the Students for a Democratic Society were as guilty as those who pulled the trigger on the victims of the My Lai slaughter. Killing is killing. I just couldn't buy it—I felt betrayed." From his point of view, the conscience of America had become, to some extent, tarnished, if not downright corrupted. He would have to dig deeper within himself for a pure, honest approach—a means of communicating truth with integrity and consistency. "Or maybe I'm being too self-righteous," he conjectured to himself, the lurching bus temporarily distracting him from his troubled thoughts.

John slumped in his seat, pulled the heavy collar of his sheepskin coat up around his neck, and closed his eyes, wishing for sleep as the vehicle slowed to navigate the streets of a small suburb on the outskirts of Detroit. Peering out the frozen window he fixed his sleepy gaze on a maze of tall stones that stretched out in a uniform network. It was the town cemetery.

Death. He was reminded of the growing toll this hard-living business had exacted from some of his contemporaries: Jimi Hendrix, Jim Morrison, and half a dozen other shining lights snuffed out prematurely.

And there was Janis Joplin. She was, in the estimation of some, the most exciting female figure in the world of rock 'n' roll. Her raspy, wailing voice and fifth of whiskey had become her trademarks. She appeared hard, but John saw the other side of her one night after a concert when they shared the billing. He remembered her conversation—halting and self-conscious, full of four-letter expletives. They were backstage, the air was blue with cigarette smoke and the pungent smell of pot. Janis took another belt from her nearly empty bottle and joked with the band. But she was really just a lost little girl. John could see it in her darkened, hungry eyes which searched for approval. She didn't look "long for this world." Still, John and Terry were stunned when word of her death by a drug overdose reached them.

Perhaps the tragedies were striking too close to home, for by this time the members of Mason Proffit were themselves experiencing the worldly joys of, shall we say, pharmacological pursuits, along with their "roadies" and local booking agents—with the sole exception of John.

"In the early days of the Mason Proffit tours there was some dope-smoking. It wasn't much. Later on, cocaine began to find its way into our recording sessions. If you listen—closely, you'll hear the record where it first happens—it was on *Last Night I Had the Strangest Dream*. Despite its pointed antiwar social comment, musically it becomes extremely spacey because the guys were doing a lot of cocaine."

I put the obvious question to him. "What about you? Were you into drugs at this point?"

"No. I never participated."

"Why not?"

"I don't know."

"Amazing."

"Yeah. I think somehow God was protecting me—I didn't seem to need the stuff."

"How involved did the others get?"

"Well, one particular evening stands out in my mind. Usually when the guys did dope they were very careful about what they used. On this one occasion they bought what they thought was cocaine, but later it was found the stuff was pretty heavily cut with heroin. Of course, they snorted a bunch of this concoction. I can still remember carrying the guys onto the bus half-paralyzed, unable to walk or talk after our concert. I found this situation very upsetting.

"What was happening, you see, is these guys were trying to do narcotics moderately, but they were getting in deeper and deeper. The music was getting worse and worse, with a 'coked-out blues' sound. Of course, the guys thought they were getting better, which is the sad part.

"It seemed like when we rode those buses there were three things to do—read, sleep, or get stoned. So the guys would go to the back of the bus to get loaded and I would sit up in front reading. After a while the whole thing began to seem like a real dead-end proposition."

That cemetery passing by the window said it all. Death seemed to be hanging in the air, riding on the shoulders of pop music's privileged elite. John's thoughts drifted into the past again, this time to memories of a darkened, smoke-filled tavern where he watched Phil Ochs and Arlo Guthrie shooting pool. Everyone was drunk. Talking about his late father, the great Woodie Guthrie, Arlo was overcome by tears. Phil was later to commit suicide.

Indeed, the memories were disquieting. Senseless tragedy and pain seemed to pervade the lives of his fellow musicians. Of course, there were those who said, with a kind of fatalistic detachment, that "it all comes with the turf." Maybe so. But then, perhaps this isn't my turf, John speculated to himself. Life is too precious, too short. There must be more to it all. There *must* be.

Without breaking his rambling chain of thought, he reached down and pulled an old, ragged Bible from his tattered leather bag. His grandmother had given it to him years before. There might be some comfort in its pages. He had begun reading it on the road, along with books on Buddhism, Hinduism, and American Indian religions. He opened the book to a heavily underlined passage and began to read, a circular beam from the overhead reading light illuminating the pages in front of him: "For what is a man profited if he gains the whole world, and loses himself?" The words of Christ echoed in his haunted soul, the question burned in his mind, demanding an answer. The bus rolled on into the damp, chilly night.

"As I try to recall that time in my life, events seem to flow into one another. It was a hard time, but also very positive because at least I was honestly searching for the truth," John says. "This quest began just about the time I was taking a second look at the so-called revolutionaries; those I had come to regard with some suspicion because they were often so crassly inconsistent with their ideals. It was also a time when many lives were crumbling all around me. I would say to myself, these people aren't happy—they're miserable. And I began packing a substantial amount of reading material to carry around with me, mostly philosophy and religion, hoping to encounter something meaningful. I would say I had begun to develop a positively universal sense of God."

John read widely within the field of religion. He began to understand man's quest for meaning and significance in various cultural settings. He related very well, for example, to the mystical and meditative qualities found in Eastern religions, recalling from his childhood moments of solitude and the sounds of God within. But he also found the nature-filled stories of the American Indian religion satisfying in a more earthy sense. "We had special feelings about the Indians anyway," John adds. "They really epitomized our cry for justice in our music. We thought, 'Hey, these are the first real Americans—the Native American people—and look what we've done to them.' I admired them for their culture, their beliefs, and their legends. It became a real cause for me and, of course, for the band."

John remembers attempting to convey some of his own growing spiritual enthusiasm to others in the band, with only limited success. "That night we were riding in the bus and Arty was drumming with his drumsticks on the metal rail around the seat cushion. I tried to tell him, as I read my Bible, that I believed God could be found if we would just search him out with sincerity. He just stared at me with an empty, blank expression on his face and said, 'Drums. Drums are the answer, man.' And he went back to beating on the metal railing, lost in his own spaced-out world of rhythm."

John would later admit that his own developing concept of God was still somewhat nebulous at this point. He didn't know whether to think of God as a he, a she, or an it, as a force or as a source of a force. "I didn't care—I just wanted to know, so I really plunged into reading, studying, and times of deep prayer. It was in that prayer experience that the pieces of the puzzle, so to speak, began to fall together into a recognizable picture—a direction in which to move."

He began to feel, with a forceful inner conviction, that there was something, or someone, above, beyond, and greater than the quagmire of unhappiness and competing egos surrounding him. There was a sense of impending revelation. He could feel it about to happen— something special, something to conclusively reward his diligent search. He could never have guessed how overpowering it would actually prove to be.

It happened in 1971, in a Holiday Inn, of all places. For an experience that would prove so immensely important in his life, John is surprisingly vague about specifics, such as the date and location of the event. "Things now rush together in my memory about those years, probably because the endless touring and performing lulled me into a stupefied indifference about where I was or when I was there, and, of course, there were far more important matters on my mind at the time," John points out. "All I remember about the general circumstances is that we were in the middle of a tour, probably somewhere in the Midwest, and spending this particular night in a Holiday Inn. I had my own room—the walls I recall as being blue—probably matched my disposition at the time."

The other band members and road crew were checking into their rooms down the hall as John closed the door and collapsed on the double bed, turning his tired gaze toward the window. The soft eerie glow of the neon hotel sign filtered softly through the drawn blue drapery, bathing him in a pattern of light and shadows. As had become his custom when there were quiet, restful moments at hand, John began to pray to a God he did not really know but had come to believe in. Almost imperceptibly, his silent, interior meditation became an audible, vocal question: "Lord, who are you?"

Then it happened. Light seemed to fill the room, intensifying by degrees as if controlled by an unseen rheostat. Startled, John sat up, blinking his eyes, assessing the situation. There before him, in mind-bending brilliance, was the figure of a man in white robes, arms outstretched, with long hair and a beard. "I saw an image," John says, "that looked like Jesus—it was a typical Christ figure—an incredible sight." A surge of adrenaline tore through his body like a hot rushing current, yet there was no fear or panic.

John recalls, "He didn't say anything—he was just there. I felt in him a sense of awesome power, overwhelming strength, yet the capacity to be very, very gentle. I felt that he could judge me in my smallness and sinfulness, but I also perceived his forgiveness. He stood before me, somehow almost *around* me, in infinite greatness yet total humility. I felt compassion. And I felt acceptance. I had been reading *about* Jesus and feeling him *in my heart*, but at that moment I actually *experienced his touch*. I knew it was Jesus."

John now refers to this event simply as "the vision." He has repeated the story a thousand times. Some people have challenged John with the suggestion that perhaps his vision was some kind of hallucination or dream. He shrugs off the skepticism claiming that, in any case, he does not necessarily hold to a miraculous manifestation of the risen Christ, explaining that God is the Lord of our psychoemotional lives and can wondrously intervene in every realm of our experience. The specific origins of the apparition, whether they be psychological, dream-induced, or externally real, have no bearing on the legitimacy of the event in John's mind.

"I experienced a positive change in my life. I felt deep love for others, forgiveness, tenderness, new levels of compassion, as if I had somehow absorbed these qualities from the Christ figure in the vision. I suppose you could say I became a Christian again. I rediscovered something from my childhood faith. I felt that it completed me as a human being. I became a better brother, in the broad sense of the word, to my friends and to the band. I didn't go back and scream at them for smoking dope. I just didn't smoke dope. After the vision, I also began to question the frenzy we worked people into from the stage, so I began to bring a bit more folk influence into the band—a bit more of an artistic emphasis. I felt the others in the band really understood me and respected me for my developing convictions. We had good conversations."

John was never the same after that evening at the Holiday Inn. Like Mary after the Annunciation, John pondered these things in his heart, speaking to no one about the vision for some time. He nourished the budding new life within by even more intensive Bible study and deeper times of meditative prayer. But love is hard to hide, and before long those around him felt its warmth. They could see that something had changed. "I think they could see the acceptance, the simple love, and the forgiveness that had become the driving forces of my life—I was in the midst of a conversion," he says.

By 1972, Mason Proffit had reached its peak. All the energy of the record industry, the media, the public, and the developing skill of the musicians themselves had come together into that rare combination for big-time success. It appeared as though there was no stopping the upward spiral of this team of individuals who, judging from outward appearances, had it all together.

In retrospect, however, John believes that just as the band looked its strongest and big-time success seemed just around the corner, the beginning of the end was at hand. There were a number of factors at work, each of which chipped away at the dream.

There is no doubt that the rough life-style, including increasing drug abuse by certain members of the group, contributed to discipline problems. And there was the general malaise experienced after having to be "up" for weeks at a time during tortuous itineraries around the country—a tiring, abrasive routine that could rub tempers raw.

However, the most significant challenges to the group's survival were artistic concerns, according to John. "Our management wanted a marketable, more commercial sound that they thought would sell more records and pump up the demand for appearances. Of course, their interests were financial, not social or artistic. I felt that we should move more toward artistic expressions of folk, bluegrass, and ethnic forms of music in order more creatively to integrate ourselves into the rock idiom. Our management, on the other hand, was pushing more toward basic mainstream rock, and we resisted that."

The underlying problems, however, were a bit more complex than band versus management. There were also divergent opinions within the group itself that began boiling to the surface that same year. "Some of our guys were really getting into jazz and blues and were getting bored with the kind of music we were known for. I wanted a mellower sound, while Terry was headed into a more hard-driving rock 'n' roll mode. So it's understandable that these creative tensions would have a divisive influence on the band. You put all these things together and you begin to have some real problems."

Indeed, it was beginning to look as though irreconcilable differences would split the group.

It was with a growing doubt about the professional direction of Mason Proffit that John returned home to Nancy after a string of concerts on the West Coast. It was February 1973. With question marks about the band looming in his mind, he had turned to prayer and to his deepening spiritual journey for consolation. And it seemed more important now than ever that things on the domestic front should work out.

There was a lump in his throat as he turned his key in the front door lock, braced against the bone-chilling wind and rain. He stepped into the dimly lit living room, a rush of warm air welcoming him as he quietly closed the door behind him. "Mustn't wake Nancy up," he thought. But before he could shed his heavy wet coat, she appeared in the hallway squinting into the living-room light.

"John. Hi, what time is it? I guess I fell asleep."

"It's a little after two. How ya doin', Nance?" They embraced, standing silently together for a long moment.

"How were the concerts?"

"Oh, they were okay—well, not really. I mean, it feels like we're just going through the motions. The guys don't have their hearts in the music anymore, not like they used to. Terry and I talked for a long time after the last performance and he's feeling the same way. We discussed the idea of working together, the two of us, if things don't pan out with Mason Proffit. We could just be the Talbot Brothers, or something." Nancy could see that he wasn't happy. There was a heaviness in his voice that she had rarely heard.

"Maybe things will come together for Mason Proffit, John. Every band has its downers," she reassured him with little confidence in her voice. "Besides, you have the Ozark Mountain Folk Fair to look forward to on the tour this spring."

He winced at the thought. They were booked so far ahead—the tunnel looked so long. The weight of it seemed unbearable.

"Nancy, you need to know—I want out of the band. I really can't stand it any more. I wouldn't be truly honest with myself, or with the other band members, if I tried to stay on for the sake of the show."

If there was one thing Nancy had come to respect about her husband, it was his resolute, uncompromising desire to be, as he had just said, honest with himself and others. Sometimes it even frightened her a little because John's deeply held convictions were often not shared by her. She knew that someday, and maybe in the not so distant future, it would become a serious matter of conflict between them. In the end, she knew that John would have to be, as he said, true to himself, and totally honest with her.

But for now they shared a warm, comforting embrace—a few silent moments together. Only the sound of a cold, winter wind could be heard raking across the roof in a low, mournful howl.

As spring approached, warm breezes coaxed blossoms from the cherry trees, and the sweet scent of the slowly greening forests of the Ozark Mountains filled the air. The sounds of saws and axes could be heard echoing through the crisp morning chill of Eureka Springs, Arkansas, as preparations were underway for the first Ozark Mountain Folk Fair, the brainchild of local entrepreneur Edd Jeffords. His director of operations, Bill O'Neill, was working feverishly with his crew to clear an amphitheatre area in the woods at Oak Hill Ecopark, ten miles north of town on Highway 23. In keeping with Jeffords's ecological ideals, many trees were left standing while the rest were used to build the stage and the arts-and-crafts booths around the perimeter of the grounds.

Edd and his wife, Linda, and a handful of friends, including the Rolling Stones' stage manager, Ted Jones, had worked for more than a year to put together a colossal music-and-arts fair, scheduled for Memorial Day weekend, 1973. It was to be the first in a series. Top-rated bands and artists were slated to participate. Sharing top billing with Mason Proffit were such greats as the Nitty Gritty Dirt Band, the Earl Scruggs Revue, John Hartford and the Ozark Mountain Daredevils. Also booked were John D. Loudermilk, Mancy Lipscomb, Johnny Shines, Kenneth Threadgill and the Velvet Cowpasture, Zydeco King, Leo Kottke, John Lee Hooker, the James Cotton Blues Band, and "Big Mama" Thornton. It would be a wild and free celebration. Local merchants were not enthusiastic, but consoled themselves with hopes of hearing the uninterrupted ringing of cash registers.

"I can honestly say that this was the peak of our career," John states confidently. "In spite of our problems, we pulled ourselves together for that festival. It felt like the old days once again. We were more than ready.

"There was a vague sense of finality going into that weekend," John remembers. It was as if the whole band knew that this would be their last big performance together, but the subject was never broached as they flew over Missouri and into northern Arkansas. They talked about the scenic rolling mountains and the beautiful countryside.

"Damn! Look at this place," Tim Ayres exclaimed, hanging his shaggy head out of the window of their rented car. Some of the guys had been looking at land just outside Tucson, but had been having second thoughts about living out in the desert. This seemed a much more attractive option and was well within financial reach.

"So we said, 'Let's buy some land—if we use it, fine, and if we don't, fine.' We knew it would be a safe investment in any case. Once we pulled into Eureka Springs, we knew this was the place. We checked into the Crescent Hotel, where most of the other acts were also registered, and settled in for the weekend," John recalls. "It was so nice out, I went out on the hotel lawn for a breath of fresh air, and just lingered out there for a long time, drinking in the view which overlooked the Saint Elizabeth of Hungary Catholic Church. By the way,

Saint Elizabeth of Hungary was the patroness of the Third Order of Saint Francis, which I didn't know at the time, of course. Ironically, I did not know that Saint Elizabeth's was a Catholic church, either. I now find this a highly symbolic incident in my life, pointing toward something I could never have dreamed at the time.

"I remember it was early evening and I was so relaxed, looking out over the landscape, that church, the statue of Jesus and the Sacred Heart. I closed my eyes and breathed a prayer and I just felt the Lord say very distinctly within my innermost heart, 'You will buy land here and someday you're going to live here.' The very next day we contacted a realtor, Clell McClung, who I later learned was one of the most active parishioners in Saint Elizabeth's, and we scoped out the area. Then and there, Terry and I bought a couple pieces of land. Two of our road managers even bought in. It was a beautiful wooded valley, nestled between high, rolling hills. It felt strangely like home to me—it was a kind of déjà vu sensation. I knew it was right."

It was half-past seven on Friday evening, May 25. The sun was setting behind the Ozarks and the folk fair was officially underway. Thousands of vehicles converged on little Eureka Springs—campers, trucks, vans, dozens of bikers with their wild-looking Harley choppers and a whole lot more out-of-state license plates than the locals had ever seen at one time. Architect-professor Robert Austin was the master of ceremonies and rolled out the carpet to one band after another. The jubilantly receptive crowd had grown to well over ten thousand and appeared to one local-newspaper reporter like "a swaying sea of blue denim."

Paul Johnson of the *Arkansas Gazette* called the event "a multisensory experience." He reported:

> Long after John Lee Hooker had concluded an extended performance with shouts of "Y'all want to boogie wit' de Hook?" the boy with hair to his waist stood alone, arms above his head, body swaying, shouting, "I wanna

boogie!" Ten minutes later, when two visitors passed him again he was rooted to the same spot, arms still extended, body still swaying, still shouting, "I wanna boogie!"

Whether his enthusiasm was brought about by marijuana, excitement over the blues and bluegrass music, or simply the good feeling that abounded at the first Ozark Mountain Folk Fair would be hard to say. All three were to be found in abundance.

The boisterous throng eventually swelled to more than thirty thousand. Almost every type of intoxicant and narcotic could be found in the place; cocaine, grass, alcohol, and more were eagerly and openly consumed. "The huge natural amphitheater seemed from some distance away like a suddenly awakened volcano," reported Johnson, referring to the marijuana fog that settled over the valley. Watermelon and corn on the cob were hawked by young vendors and it seemed that cases of beer were stacked by the ton near all the concession stands.

Chief of Police Lee Roy Weems, Jr., was astounded at the dimensions of the traffic jam, but was prepared for any emergency with medical equipment, ambulances, and watchful cops, who arrested a token forty-two people for drug or weapons violations. Aside from several bad acid trips and minor overdoses, few medical emergencies arose, with the exception of one young lady who was bitten by a copperhead snake.

The crowd was treated to a rollicking good time of earsplitting music performed by the country's leading experts in folk-rock. It was an experience none would forget, with a hot sound setup provided by the Showco Company of Little Rock and the amphitheater's acoustical effects saturated the air with pounding, rhythmic music for miles.

Steve Vanhook of the *Times-Echo* newspaper noted that the Earl Scruggs Revue was a highlight, judging by the crowd's applause for the "King of Banjo." The Dirt

Band was also a hit, teaming up with Hartford and Scruggs for a show-stopping jam session. The most generous comments by critics, however, were reserved for Mason Proffit. In the words of one reporter, "The hit act was Mason Proffit, a foot-stomping, bluegrass-rock band that had the crowd shouting back responses to shouted questions. The act ended with the lead singer advising the crowd not to lose the good feeling that was evident on the hillside. 'When some guy starts beating you on the head,' he advised the crowd, 'just give him a big wide grin; it drives them crazy!'" Apparently, Terry couldn't resist a short sermon between numbers.

Years later, Terry would discover that his best childhood friend from Little Rock, Wally Lovelace, was in the crowd. "Wally, now a successful real-estate broker, was right there in the front row, clapping, dancing—having a high old time. The funny thing is that I never saw him and he didn't recognize me. Only years later, when he came to see one of my Christian concerts, did we put two and two together," Terry says. "It was a truly amazing experience!"

When John and Terry stepped up to their microphones with their banjo and guitar and began to sing the ballad, "Two Hangmen," the crowd burst into unrestrained applause, then just as quickly hushed themselves to listen, some singing along quietly. "Eugene Pratt," an anti-Vietnam war comment, stirred up the masses as its melody drifted out through the valley. When John began "Sail Away," he brought the throng to their feet. The band closed their set only to be shouted back to the stage.

John remembers surveying the crowd, seeing them as a lost flock of sheep looking for a leader, searching for an answer. "There was an awful lot of dope, free lovemaking, nudity, drunkenness—I felt a deep caring and compassion for them. Even as I played and sang, even as I felt that old stage rush of adrenaline, I was at the same time stricken with a kind of grief." He learned a little about how Jesus felt when a crowd of thousands looked to him for sustenance, and he fed them all with one boy's lunch of bread and fish.[1] "Let me be obedient and giving, like that boy in the Gospel story," John whispered prayerfully as he scanned the more than thirty thousand festival participants. "Let me somehow feed people with the truth, with the bread of life."

Musically, the band had never performed better. "We were at the peak of our career," John repeats. "We had a very tight seven-member band with a top lead guitarist, a mellotrone[2] player who doubled on harmonica and piano, a fiddler who doubled on mandolin and guitar—we had it all together for the best sound we ever made. I doubled on dobro, banjo, guitar, and pedal steel. We sang four-part harmonies, did a lot of acoustical stuff, bluegrass, and a fair amount of rock 'n' roll."

For many of the musicians, the event was a kind of nostalgic reunion. The Mason Proffit guys had performed with the Nitty Gritty Dirt Band in Aspen, they knew the Scruggs people from Nashville, and had encountered most of the others from their years of travel around the country. So it seemed only natural as the folk fair drew to a close that they should all gather on stage on the final evening for a grand finale of folk and bluegrass standards, capped with a last song, "Will the Circle Be Unbroken?"

For John, it was to be a special event, marking, in a way, the end of an era for him, leaving bittersweet memories of the Mason Proffit band at its all time best.

As he loaded his gear and prepared to depart for Indiana, John paused, inhaling the fresh mountain air laden with the fragrances that herald the onset of summer in the Arkansas forests. He turned toward the horizon and stared at the huge figure that dominated the Eureka Springs skyline and had become one of the area's main tourist draws: an immense statue with outstretched arms, a beard, long hair. It was the legendary Christ of the Ozarks.

Chapter Five

Breaking Up

"The 1973 Ozark Mountain Folk Fair is still remembered in Eureka Springs; in fact, the place will probably never be the same because of it," John muses, fingering the tattered newspaper clippings that have yellowed over a decade. "That event led to other festivals and concerts, and, I think, brought some folks permanently into the Eureka Springs area who would otherwise have never come. Some of the arts-and-crafts shops and counterculture communities trace their presence all the way back to that fair. I really feel that for many it was a kind of watershed experience, me included. I couldn't forget about Eureka Springs, but as things were later to turn out, I couldn't think about returning either, because of all that was happening in my life."

The land he had purchased would serve from time to time as a pleasant reminder that he had a piece of "paradise" awaiting him in the future—maybe someday he would return, he thought, and build a ranch or small farm. He could grow his own food, write music, and raise a family in the woods of the Ozarks. This was an image he would cherish for years, and would call upon for consolation in the months following the folk fair, as the life of the itinerant rock band began to dissolve like a dream at dawn's first light.

Perhaps it was more of a nightmare than a dream. After months of agonizing about the band and about his own journey in life, John pulled the plug on Mason Proffit and, along with his brother, quit.

The Mason Proffit string of success had, shall we say, stopped vibrating. Not only were the band members moving in different directions artistically, but increased drug abuse was taking a massive toll on creativity and energy levels. They were losing the touch—and the ambition—for big-league success. John felt he could no longer contribute to the band, or even fit in, for that matter.

Attendance levels at Mason Proffit concerts became unpredictable, with ten thousand ticket holders one night, two thousand the next—a situation extremely unattractive to promoters and agents. It wasn't that the music or the actual performances of the band had deteriorated drastically. The real problem was a lack of sensitivity to the audiences, undoubtedly due to a combination of factors, not the least of which was temperamental, dissatisfied band members who were "coked-out" on stage.

Today, Terry winces at the memories. "Yeah, I was into drugs and was adversely affected by those experiences. Toward the end of the Mason Proffit era I was doing half a gram of cocaine and half a bottle of tequila every day." Obviously, something had to give. And it did.

When John and Terry finally left the group, Mason Proffit became history, even before their Warner Brothers recording contract had expired. One album remained to be produced, so John and Terry put their heads together and came up with a plan. "Here we were with an album to record and no Mason Proffit," recalls John. "So we cut an album—Terry and I. Finally we got together with Warner Brothers and handed them this record saying, 'Oh, by the way, this is a Talbot brothers album, not Mason Proffit.'"

John and Terry hit the road to promote the album but understandably received very little support from Warner Brothers. An album that contained some very good material died what the Talbot brothers considered a premature death. "It was an excellent album, called *The Talbot Brothers: Reborn.* We used Randy and Gary Scruggs, Russ Kunkle on drums, and Leland Sklar on bass. It was a beautiful album—we did our best vocals ever on that record. And another thing—Terry had become a Christian during that time. It was right during that time that Terry became very serious about his commitment to Christ."

Suddenly John is telling me that his coke-snorting, tequila-drinking, stage-swaggering brother is a Christian. Of course, I had to dig into this a bit deeper, and ultimately got to know and appreciate Terry Talbot, an extremely talented individual who still possesses that charisma and charm from the early days of pumping up audiences into exuberant celebration.

I asked Terry to share the story of his conversion. "Well, Dan, you know I've just gotta say that John's conversion really had an influence on me—a very positive one. He was so deeply and totally committed to God, and I sincerely wanted to be that committed to something." Terry paused to collect his thoughts and continued, "In 1971 I began to think a lot about spiritual things and finally, in '73, I made that total commitment to actually living a truly Christian life. I stopped the coke and booze cold turkey and never went back. Thank God."

Terry's journey was similar to John's in that he rationally thought through his questions and searched for answers in various religious traditions. "I found that several religions honor the Bible and biblical tradition," he explains. "And many of the world's peoples acknowledge the unique role that Jesus played in history as a prophet, even though they may not, in fact, consider him to be the Son of God. In the final analysis, I was overwhelmed by Jesus Christ, for all he *was* and *is*. I was particularly overpowered by the total mercy of his incarnation—the fact that, for us, he became a man."

Terry glows as he relates his transformation, his enthusiasm still strong after more than a decade of following the man from Galilee. His evangelistic zeal is, in some ways, perhaps even more apparent today, as growing personal confidence and deepening commitment seem to energize his life both on and off the stage. He still preaches, just like in the old days. The difference is that now Terry has what he consideres a viable solu-

tion to offer to a troubled generation, and he does so
through his music.

One of the consequences of the Talbot brothers' conversion to faith in Christ was a sudden proliferation of
songs that testify to their changed lives and philoso-
phies. Their first album as a duo for Warner Brothers
bears a distinctly Christian mark, particularly in the cut
"Hear You Callin'":

> I hear you callin' me,
> I hear you callin',
> in the weepin' of the willow tree
> at dawn.
>
> Jesus, how I believe in you,
> can't keep from cryin' when I think
> of all the pain you knew,
> for so long.
>
> And you know I will always stand beside
> you,
> you know I will always keep your light
> growin' in my mind.
>
> Oh, I hear you callin' me,
> I hear you callin',
> in the weepin' of the willow tree
> at dawn.[1]

Although the energy of personal conversion is
clearly transmitted through this album, the social concern still breaks through. In another cut, "Trail of Tears,"
John laments the fate of the American Indians, hearken-
ing back "to Wounded Knee to count the dead."
Throughout his career John had maintained the remark-
able ability to empathize with the oppressed through his
music.

As the riot-torn sixties and early seventies became
more subdued—some would say, more apathetic—the
Talbots, now fervently professing Christ as "born again"
believers, had rekindled their own spirits with an inter-

nal revolution that would demand more focused, prayerful attention. Not long after their last Warner Brothers album, they withdrew from the recording scene to seek, to search, to press on with their individual journeys. John, already a bookworm, immersed himself even deeper in reading and study.

"First of all, let me point out something," John says. "This was a very positive time in my Christianity—it was purely and simply a wonderful experience and I wanted to know more about everything surrounding it." He and Nancy were living in Munster, Indiana, following the split of Mason Proffit. With the demise of the group now behind him, he felt a new freedom to pursue his budding faith on an almost full-time basis. "We were attending a typical Methodist church, and, of course, I sought counsel and teaching from the pastor, who gave me Barclay's Bible commentaries to read. Later, I began spending time with an American Baptist pastor who became a very definite inspiration in my life." John found the pastor to be very open, and active in the charismatic renewal. John learned as much as he could, as fast as he could, and, like the banjo teachers who were quickly outpaced by his bursting musical abilities, the pastors who counseled him had soon almost exhausted their theological reservoirs.

"What about the so-called 'Jesus movement,' which was in full swing then? Were you involved?" I asked.

"No, not really. Of course, I knew about it, but I can't say I was part of it. I was a renewal-oriented Christian. If I were to use a label, 'renewal' would be the word."

"Does this mean you were charismatic?"

"No, not necessarily, although a little later on I had that experience without even knowing what it was."

"Explain."

"Well, I was on a plane, gazing out a window at the clouds and thinking, I've seen clouds from both sides, you know, like the Joni Mitchell song. I was just daydreaming—I can't even remember where I was flying to—but I found myself praising God for the beauty of his creation. It was like I was drawn up to God in some kind of meditative state of worship. I don't know how long I was in it, but I was singing joyfully, with a new melody and a new language, oblivious to everything around me. Suddenly I became rather self-conscious and looked around to see this businessman in a three-piece suit looking at me, smiling and nodding. I smiled and nodded back and began looking at the clouds again. Somehow I wasn't the same after that. I felt I was flooded with the Holy Spirit."

John admits that he was skeptical about the charismatic movement. He denied, for a time, his charismatic experience, but later acknowledged its place in his life, as his studies confirmed the historical validity of this dimension of spiritual renewal—even in the more traditional churches. He found in his reading, for example, that the Franciscans, when praying together, had sometimes fallen over on the ground, as if asleep, for hours under the power of the Spirit's presence. "I even read that Saint Anthony, a Franciscan, once preached a sermon in tongues and people of different languages heard the message in their own language—just as in the Book of Acts," John relates. "I began to feel more comfortable about my own experience in light of this."

John says that at this point, not long after his conversion, his personal direction was a "Spirit-led, Spirit-filled, Christ-centered walk with God." It seems, however, that just as a mountaintop is bordered by the inevitable plunge into a valley, our life experiences are a never-ending chain of victories and defeats, highs and lows, that challenge our preconceptions and shake our complacency. We are forced to reexamine the path of life on which we walk. This was certainly the case with John.

"I found myself heading toward a crisis point," he says. "Here I am, this young Christian, I'm not trained theologically, I'm not really locked into a single church, yet I'm desperately hungry for more of God. I'm looking for true spiritual authority to submit myself to." He began reading with a vengeance—the Bible, commentaries, and books by Francis Schaeffer, Dietrich Bonhoeffer, Hal Lindsey, and a host of others, many of whom had a strong fundamentalist bent.

"I was reading, consuming, grasping. I was beginning to lose that open, simple love. I was living in a subtle kind of fear; a fear that said 'You don't know all you need to know.' I was made to feel that I had to memorize a lot of Scripture before I could be truly accepted by my Christian brothers and sisters. It was a smothering sort of spiritual self-consciousness."

Over the next months, John surrounded himself with a wall of books that became for him a virtual prison, as real as his childhood jailhouse trauma. He had been exposed to fundamentalist Christianity, which, in its dogmatic certainty and zeal, represented a kind of false harbor of security. He had a clear, rigid set of rules to live by and doctrinal explanations that provided a sense of stability and definition for a world that was unstructured and full of change.

"I began to push the Bible too legalistically. Slowly, but very surely, I became a walking, talking Jesus freak who had a quote from Scripture for every conceivable problem. I really entered into what I call a caricature of Christianity rather than a full, beautiful painting of Jesus, with vibrant color, subtle shadow, power, and gentleness. At this stage of things I believed as I was taught: that this particular brand of Christianity, narrow as it was, represented the only real truth. Everyone else was just a little off, except Catholics, who were way off. I was exposed to the view that Catholicism is the great whore of Babylon, an evil religion that was prophesied in the Bible to emerge in the 'end times.' I was extremely anti-Catholic at that time. I was like a misrepresentation of Christ—like a black-and-white cartoon.

"I would visit old friends, like our band members, and come on like a Bible thumper, condemning their life-styles and spitting out Scripture verses to make my point. I scared them to death! I know they were thinking, 'Hey, John boy, you've changed. You're not the loving, patient friend you were before.' And they were absolutely right."

He was argumentative, and his prodigious reading had left him with an impressive vocabulary and an array of theological weapons for every occasion. He could leave some poor soul sputtering and stammering with a wounded spirit and damaged faith. In more debates than he cares to remember he would convert his opponent to his own fundamentalist position. "I talked more Catholics out of their church—it was frightening. I convinced them they couldn't really be saved in the Catholic church with all that idol worship and repeated ritual. Sometimes I scared even me!"

Nancy, too, was disturbed. "Who is this person I'm living with?" she wondered to herself. Obviously, she had trouble relating to John because she had not subjected herself to the same rigorous study. She just knew something was wrong—and getting worse. And she didn't like it.

Initially, she had followed John into a relationship with Christ that eventually became her own genuine experience. The catch came, however, when she realized that the path she was following as she sincerely attempted to live out her own expression of Christianity was diverging from John's more intense approach. The common faith that should have brought them closer together was, ironically, driving them even farther apart.

But there was more to the problem than conflicting religious views. John, for the first time since the age of ten, was out of work, and this created turbulent undercurrents in the months following his last record with Terry. Moreover, he could not admit to having very real doubts and fears because of his notion that a truly dedicated Christian should have "victory" over all challenges. In essence, to admit depression or fear would be to admit failure as an "overcoming" believer. He felt he had to have a handle on every problem—or, at least, project that image—to be worthy of Christ. All this simply compounded the battle that was being waged in his own troubled spirit.

"It was a rugged time," John admits. "I wasn't really working, just painting houses to bring in some money. I grew a garden and would go around the neighborhood with sacks full of green beans to sell to neighbors for a few extra dollars—a big change for a guy who only a couple years earlier was out singing to twenty thousand people and earning real good money. And that had to be difficult for Nancy to deal with. After all, she married a successful rock 'n' roll star, and all of a sudden she's confronted with this seeking, searching, almost flipping-out poor Christian man. Big change. But I have to say, she hung in there with me when most women would have called it quits."

He began barricading himself against his topsy-turvy world with his Bible and books, rarely venturing out for a breath of fresh air. But try as he might, John could not reclaim the peace and power that had been his in the wake of the vision.

"It was like I was losing my heart," he remembers. "I was jamming my head full of theological facts and passages of Scripture while all the time losing my grip on love, on Christ himself. I was fighting a battle for my own spiritual life and didn't even know it!"

It was as though the clear, singular voice of Jesus was being drowned out by a cacophony of urgent appeals. The final spiritual authority he sought seemed to lead him to the Bible, but, as John now freely admits, the Bible became an idol in itself. "I was becoming more centered on that book than on Jesus," he claims. "I was unwittingly committing the sin of bibliolatry."

With a faltering marriage, lack of work, and an increasingly confused approach to his Christian faith, John found himself in a spiritual desert. His own conscience even turned against him: Can I play rock music and still be a Christian? Should I even play music at all? And what about ecology? Should I drive a car, pollute the environment, deplete petroleum reserves, and contribute to an evil system based on greed and power? And what about diet? Shouldn't we as Christians eat only natural foods, and only certain natural foods, like vegetables and grains? He was seized violently by fits of scrupulosity—indeed, self-condemnation seemed to stalk him at every turn. He sunk into a maze of ethical and philosophical questions from which he could not break loose. He had become a prisoner in his own mind. Maybe, he thought, maybe I'm going crazy.

Or perhaps it was the test to which he was put in order to explore the darker regions of his own being— the classic desert experience that seems to befall so many true believers who seek the kingdom of God. The serious pilgrim must slay his dragons, cast out his de- mons, and fell his giants. For that indefinable "dark night of the soul," as Saint John of the Cross called it, will either take your life or purge it like a refinery's fire in the private, lonely crucible of interior crisis. "It is es- pecially when it is making progress," Saint John writes, "that the soul encounters darkness and ignorance."

To Saint John of the Cross, a sixteenth-century Spanish mystic, people of true spiritual greatness were more often distinguished by darkness than by lumi- nous, spiritual assurances. (It is interesting to note that Saint John went on to build monastic communities that were dedicated to prayer and to a stark, simple life-style, a way of living to which Talbot would later be drawn.) Saint John of the Cross championed the cause of con- templative prayer when he said, "Let those who are great actives, who think to gird the world with outward works and preaching, take note here that they would bring far more profit to the church and be far more pleasing to God if they spent only half as much time abiding with God in prayer . . . assuredly, they would accomplish more with one piece of work than they do now with a thousand . . . to act otherwise is to hammer vigorously and accomplish little more than nothing, at times nothing at all—at times, indeed, it may even do harm."[2]

Eventually John would read those words and ponder their deep wisdom. He would also study the writings of Thomas Merton, a Trappist monk who echoed for the modern world Saint John's call to contemplation: "We will communicate only the contagion of our own obsessions, our aggressiveness, our egocentric ambitions, our delusions about ends and means, our doctrinaire prejudices and ideas. We have more powers at our disposal today than we ever had, yet we are more alienated and estranged from the inner ground of meaning and love than we have ever been."[3]

Merton's answer for our problem is reflective, meditative prayer. This was the tool with which the troubled young musician would begin to pull himself toward reality, toward sanity, toward faith. In the midst of his shaken world, John began silently and regularly to pray deep, simple prayers. It was as though he were starting over, with the image of Christ still in his memory from the vision occupying the central position in his anxious thoughts.

In the spring of 1974, John's strength began to grow. It was early May and he was out alone for a walk on a particularly beautiful Sunday morning. He and Nancy had decided not to go to church because she wasn't feeling well—the baby was due soon and she wouldn't feel comfortable straying too far from the house. Besides, he rationalized to himself, nature and the outdoors are just as much a sanctuary as any church building. He stopped, peering down at his heavy hiking boots, then visually tracing the moss-filled cracks that marbled the concrete of the old sidewalk. He felt good about himself for the first time in ages—he seemed to have a grip on things, generally speaking. Somehow, the unresolved questions didn't seem so pressing. John breathed in the cool fresh air full of springtime and marveled at how the months had flown since the previous May, when Mason Proffit dazzled the multitudes at the Ozark Mountain Folk Fair. Now those days were gone forever; the dream had died as natural a death as the rock world is capable of dishing out. He smiled to himself as he laid it to rest once again in his mind.

And it seemed like just last week—or even yesterday morning—that he had trudged into the house from his beloved garden with huge globs of dirt on his boots. Taking them off, he shuffled toward the kitchen sink to wash his hands when Nancy fluttered in, bags of groceries awkwardly balanced in each arm.

"Did you make your doctor's appointment?" he asked absentmindedly.

"I was late, but I made it in."

"Well?"

"Well, I'm pregnant!" Nancy squealed in unrestrained delight, awaiting her stunned husband's response.

"All right!" he shrieked, dancing around the kitchen, then embracing his wife, dumping over a sack of groceries, and knocking her off balance.

"We reacted like the kids we were," John chuckles. "We were really happy with the news. There was a kind of unspoken expectation between us that this would cement our relationship for good—it would bond us together and save the marriage."

"We were so happy," Nancy recalls. "We celebrated right there in the kitchen. But deep down inside I think I also felt fear—John wasn't really working and I really wondered how we would support a growing family." Their elation temporarily overshadowed the practical concerns that would weigh upon them.

As John continued his Sunday morning walk, he laughed out loud as he caught himself unconsciously doing the rapid-breathing exercise from their natural-childbirth classes. They had decided that John would be present in the delivery room to assist in the birth. Now the time was nearly upon them. It seemed impossible that the weeks had flown so quickly.

A few hours past midnight on May 9, 1974, Amy Noel Talbot was born. John and Nancy had just finished cleaning up after his late-night birthday party. Twenty years old, and now a father—would he measure up? He thought so at the time. But he would have to do better than he did in the delivery room, where he very nearly passed out. In spite of all the preparation he just wasn't ready for the ordeal. He would be all right, he assured himself repeatedly.

He would find work. Just maybe he and Terry would get lucky with their music again. They had been collaborating off and on over the past few months, playing and writing songs. John and Nancy would occasionally fly out to California to visit Terry and his wife, Idona. They had hopes of reviving the Talbot brothers team. But it wasn't happening. The right combination had not been nailed down. Perhaps they'd get things going in the summer. "Don't hold your breath," Nancy playfully warned, only half-joking.

In the past few weeks John had been seeking the counsel of a wise American Baptist minister. It was through this series of sessions that John felt himself swinging back toward more spiritual balance in his life. He had mellowed toward those of different denominational persuasions and his harsh fundamentalist views were softening slowly. This was certainly to Nancy's relief. It seemed she had been holding her breath as John frantically tried to sort himself out spiritually. She admired the totality of his commitment to integrity and his immeasurable desire to serve the Christ he was still discovering. But he had been putting himself and those around him through nearly impossible changes—the limits of Nancy's ability to cope were quickly being reached. She had even talked with John's parents. They told her they knew that Johnny was going through a difficult phase, and, yes, they understood her situation. They would be praying and supportive. Just hang on, came the well-meaning advice. So, hang on she did— with white knuckles and all the faith she could summon to the formidable task. John's softer disposition was a welcome breath of fresh air. All she wanted was a normal family, a normal home, and normal Christianity.

"Nancy was looking for a comfortable Christian life, you know, nice clothes, nice car—standard family life. Although I was mellowing at the time, I was still asking myself, How do I live out my Christian beliefs? My beliefs were based on my perception of a Gospel that demanded simplicity, sacrifice, and total commitment. So when I would talk about living on a farm, Nancy pictured a large, modern, automated farm, while I was really thinking about a secluded little log cabin in the woods. Our ideas were just different," John explains. "My ideas were much more radical and much more simple, poorer. Hers were much more normal—I'll readily admit that. It's not that she was seeking luxury. She just wanted an average American life-style—I can't fault her for that."

It became evident to Nancy that Amy's birth was not going to change John's otherworldly ideas. The baby did indeed seem to bring them closer for a time, as together they loved, and made plans for, Amy. But it was an exterior force and not a deepening inner bonding that had driven them together. Nancy's worries about the marriage returned during the year after the baby's birth.

"To me it seemed that John was straying from reality. I tried to be supportive, to be a good loving wife. And I think I was. But John was constantly reading and writing—activities in which I was not involved. We weren't touching each other's lives anymore because he was lost in a world of spiritual things that I could not grab hold of."

John remembers discovering the crux of their crisis—that they hadn't truly understood the very idea of marriage in the first place, and this was further complicated by their extremely divergent concepts of Christianity. He shuddered at the idea of divorce or separation, although they sometimes seemed the only logical conclusions. We have to make it work, he determined.

He continued his counseling with the Baptist minister, determined to make his marriage and his Christianity work together. He sought the face of God in desperate, fervent prayer.

As in many pressured marriages, finances played a significant role. John, much to Nancy's chagrin, didn't seem to care at all about money. It even seemed to be his enemy, or at least an unnecessary complication, while she regarded it as a tool, a certain measure of security for the family and the future. One would think that record royalties, residuals, and concert receipts would have provided a hefty monetary cushion, and for a while they did. As is so often the case with successful young bands, however, funds began to disappear.

"In plain English," John recounts, "we were ripped off. We were unexpectedly caught in this tax bind and when we looked into things, far too late, we found we had really been taken advantage of. I don't want to name names—that's not important now. But those we had trusted took us for a very expensive ride. Terry and I learned some hard lessons," says John, looking back with forgiveness on the culprits.

But forgiveness doesn't pay the bills, and John began to realize he had to round up some cash. So there he sat one day in their Munster home, feet propped up on the kitchen table, rocking back in a groaning wooden chair, looking like a logger from the Yukon with his heavy, faded flannel shirt, aging Levis and well-worn, thrice-repaired high-topped boots. The phone rang, jangling the silence and very nearly upsetting the balancing act. Scrambling to the phone, John buried the receiver in his shoulder-length locks.

"John? Terry. I've got a proposition for you, little brother."

"Let's hear it."

"Well, you know we're putting Mason Proffit back together—"

"Yeah, Terry, but you know I can't really . . ."

"Wait a minute, will ya? Listen to me, now. I want you to open for us, okay? We are all singing for Jesus anyway. What do you say?"

"I say, when do we start, brother?"

"The Talbot brothers ride again! I'll call with details."

"All right. I'll get back to you."

Back on the road—and bring on the banjo, he thought with glee. And the paycheck. The time is right.

John bounced into the bedrom. Nancy was feeding Amy and wondering why he was staring at her with the gleeful grin. John shared his plans. "You and the baby could come along," he insisted. She responded with guarded optimism.

"It was about mid-1976 when Terry put the band together and back on the road," John says. "It was just small-time touring. They weren't what Mason Proffit had been, but they were good and played a circuit of bars, pubs, and auditoriums, drawing as many as three thousand or as few as a hundred. I began to open for them and I found that when I pulled out my dobro and my banjo, people loved it. I even began getting standing ovations before the band came on."

It was John's reentry into music, and it felt good. He was given the opportunity he had always wanted—to test himself as a solo performer. The response was exhilarating. It was also a chance to perform with Terry once again.

"I began to take definite steps and said, okay, I'm going to get back into this, I'm going to support my family, I'm going to be a musician. It temporarily eased the financial situation. It looked like it could really take off," says John.

On one of these tours a chance meeting changed the course of John's musical career. The new Mason Proffit had attempted to swing a deal with Arista Records that eventually fell through. The point of the exercise, however, was very clear. The Talbot brothers wanted to get back into recording, and John, in particular, wanted nothing more than to sing to the glory of God, to integrate his Christian message with musical excellence in new ways. When the Arista deal didn't pan out, John looked elsewhere in the recording industry. It was then that he met Billy Ray Hearn, an executive with Myrrh Records, a well-known Christian record label.

Billy Ray, an easygoing man with smiling eyes and a soft, engaging Texas accent, seemed the perfect person to talk to about the Christian recording business, a relatively new phenomenon generally dubbed "contemporary Christian music." John found it to be a world unto itself, with a growing constituency, its own record charts, even its own periodicals, award ceremonies, and rising stars, such as Barry McGuire, Larry Norman, Pat Boone, Jamie Owens, John Fisher, and scores of groups. Many of these entities had emerged from the Jesus movement and were now perfecting their music within their own self-contained business world.

A number of the artists were Christian celebrities, that is, entertainers with established reputations who had moved from secular to sacred music but who generally had been already regarded as stars before their involvement with Christian recording. Others could be called celebrity Christians, personalities emerging from within the Christian community and not widely known outside of the Christian music market or the church-performance circuit. John could perhaps be best seen as being among the Christian celebrities.

"When I met Billy Ray Hearn I asked him if I could make a Christian album for Myrrh," John recalls. "He seemed very interested but a bit evasive, and made no commitments at that time."

What John could not have known then was that Hearn was busily working behind the scenes to start his own record company in a bold business move that would eventually be highly successful. Sparrow Records was on the drawing boards, and while Billy Ray recognized John's talent and huge potential, he was simply not ready to let the cat out of the bag.

When the time was right, Hearn announced his plans, receiving mixed reviews, including prophesies of doom based on a depressed record market and a limited roster of artists on contract. "There was a fair amount of talk around town that Billy Ray was in over his head with Sparrow," recalls then executive vice-president of Pat Boone's Lamb and Lion Records, Doug Corbin. "A lot of people were waiting to see what would happen and, of course, we watched with great interest as he signed first one group then another to the label. It's now obvious the man has made an incredible contribution to the field, with dozens of bestselling Christian albums. Millions of lives have been touched with a Gospel message packaged in quality sound," observes Corbin, now an executive with *Contemporary Christian Music* magazine, the Bible of the Christian record business.

John Talbot was snapped up in due course. An enduring business partnership and a meaningful friendship were born. John began to record, using mostly his own material, and once more hit the road, touring the West Coast and the Midwest.

"I was finally a solo performer, doing what I really wanted, which was writing my own music, recording my own albums, and doing it all for the Lord. I was all his. And it helped the domestic situation in a limited financial way. But I would have to say that it hurt the marriage, because I was away a lot on tour. On the occasions that Nancy did come along, I would frequently play little coffee houses and prayer groups where the people were a little threatening to her in their sometimes extreme ideas. But I felt it was good—it was, in a sense, a new beginning," John concedes.

To many of those radical Christians, John was quite literally a godsend. He was an honest breath of fresh air in an increasingly commercial religious milieu. His lyrics were prophetic and challenging, but the music in which those lyrics were couched was mellow, smooth, and haunting. Talbot cut a rugged image with his worn jeans, workshirts and long—really long—hair. Many of his pictures bear a startling resemblance to pop singer Kenny Loggins. "I wanted to be about ministry, not entertainment," points out the socially conscious singer. "I found that there were still a lot of Mason Proffit carryovers in my style that, though technically correct, were nevertheless not suited to my new goals. I attempted to drive home the message with both social and spiritual content but was relying on professional techniques rather than the guiding of the Spirit. So I would set people up for a good time with an up-tempo piece, follow with a subduing series of songs, and then really drop the hammer of conviction with a haunting, serious number."

While John sensed a satisfying emotional response, he was somehow left with a feeling of spiritual emptiness. The message was not moving most people on a deeper level. His concerts at times felt like hollow victories, although sales of his new Sparrow record, *John Michael Talbot*, were encouraging. Then one day, John sat down with Barry McGuire, a Christian musician best known for his secular hit "Eve of Destruction" and his role in the Broadway musical *Hair*.

"Barry, your music touches people—it reaches people. I've seen it and I want that ability to really minister," John said. Barry sat silently, stroking his beard, squinting thoughtfully skyward. "How can I reach people?" John repeated his question.

"Well, brother, *you* don't reach people. You sing to God, you worship God and talk to God while you're onstage, and let *God* reach the people."

Barry's simple yet profound words of advice penetrated to the depths of John's heart. "Barry McGuire is very much responsible for a tremendous breakthrough in my music ministry," John affirms. "I began to encounter other artists who were living by that rule— Nancy Honeytree, Phil Keaggy, and others. Sometimes they would sing, play, and say the same things at every concert, yet people were moved deeply because it was God touching those lives."

A subsequent realization began to gnaw at John— the problem of church affiliation. By the time his second record, *New Earth*, was released, John was grappling with this issue, just another in a chain of challenges confronting him as he grew and matured in his craft and in his Christianity.

"I was becoming more popular—I had begun to worship God in my apperances, which, as a consequence, became very, very good. I was doing eighty performances a year and couldn't keep up with demand," John observes. He had become an established member of the Christian music scene by 1976. He was emerging as a leader and spokesman.

"The thing that amazed me about those other Christian artists, many of whom were becoming my friends, was that they were all rooted in a church, balanced in their ministry, and grounded in humility. In contrast, I was a loner, not submitted to ecclesiastical authority, and highly confident of my abilities, my interpretation of Scripture, my prophetic role. I began to want authority, I wanted to be humble—it was a real process of maturation for me. I continued to seek."

Things may have been developing well in John's ministry and music, but all was not well at home. Once the thrill and novelty of parenthood and of new recording contracts had worn off, he was once again confronted with the realities of a failing marriage. It was a heavy emotional burden but not one he was willing to freely share. Marriage problems were not supposed to be found among minister-musicians. After all, they were teaching and preaching to hungry crowds about how to live.

"I began to keep up a nice Christian front, you know, that I'm the together young leader. I know my Bible, I'm a charismatic, the gifts of the Spirit are working in my life. Isn't my family wonderful? Isn't my ministry successful? These ideas were like prerequisites to minister publicly. The whole time, my ministry wasn't truly what I wanted it to be, my church life wasn't what I wanted it to be, nor was my family life what I wanted it to be. Once again in this mercurial time in my life, I was in trouble. Serious trouble," John admits, referring primarily to his home life.

There was a sudden rash of divorces among leading personalities in the evangelical Christian world—especially in the music-ministry crowd. This was a terribly shocking development, not only for this network of friends, but for their growing constituencies. "I just couldn't let it happen to me," John says, still incredulous years later. "Divorce was viewed as a real scandal; I think it still is. Maybe in some ways it should be. But forgiveness was sure hard to find, even among the friends of those unfortunate enough to endure this tragedy. While divorce represents real failure and sin, and while we know that God hates divorce, we are not called to condemn these people. We are called to love."

In the midst of emotionally stormy times, of nagging self-doubt and setbacks, John held tightly to something that no one could ever take away—the vision, the reality of spiritual rebirth, the basic commitment to the loving Christ he had encountered. This was his rock, his anchor of reality, even when the Christian pursuits themselves became troubling, and, at times, even oppressive.

In John's mind, his Christian witness to the world and his well-received music ministry were on the edge of ruin. How could he continue to be a real Christian or an inspiration to others if he could not even work out his own marital problems? What if divorce is inevitable? What will the media say, what will Billy Ray think, and the parents? The questions multiplied in his troubled mind. I simply won't let it happen, he determined. It just can't.

On this note of determination he bought every book he could find on marriage and family counseling. "I began to bring home these books on sexuality, psychology, parenting—everything I could find. We read them together. We knew there had to be an answer—it was just a matter of finding it. Though things were tough, I knew we could work it out," John says, remembering his feelings during those difficult days. "I would go out on the road with this awful feeling deep inside and be away from Nancy and Amy and desperately want to get home. Once I was home things were so fragmented and tense that I would find myself wishing for the road. I needed an answer. I needed resolution."

It came sooner than he could have dreamed. "I want out, John, and I want out now," Nancy announced one day. "I want a separation. I can't handle this anymore." The words struck like bullets.

Yes, John had imagined in his worst nightmares that this was an option she might choose. Somehow it did not blunt the shock he felt through his whole being. And he knew she meant it. There would be no turning back, judging from the force of her words.

Nancy recalls those moments vividly. "I was supportive for as long as I could be. When John was going through his fundamentalist phase, I stood behind him. But after a while I lost it, and I was the one who needed support, but John couldn't provide that for me, and I understand that. Things that I couldn't buy into were matters of deep conviction for him."

Broken and heartsick, John went to live with his parents. The separation ultimately led to divorce and proved to be, without doubt, the most painful time of John's life. Over and over he would ask, How could this be happening to me? The events merged together in his mind, churning like a storm-tossed sea, flooding him with a sense of impending doom.

"I've really attempted to boil it all down in recent years and I have come to some basic conclusions," John observes with the calm of a person who has begun to mend emotionally. "Nancy was really called to be married to a good Christian man, the kind who works eight hours a day, Monday through Friday. On the other hand, I was called to be an artist, a contemplative, in some ways a poor hermit. As a musician on the road my life was erratic and somewhat unpredictable. While Nancy was meant to be a good middle-American housewife, I felt strongly called to a more radical life-style."

Nancy has since remarried. She and John see one another on occasion and engage in frequent phone conversations, usually regarding Amy. "There has been real healing between us," John assures. "I consider Nancy and her husband close friends."

As John reviews this very difficult time in his life, he offers some thoughts that he believes could assist others as they consider marriage and family life. "I feel strongly that marriage, like celibacy, should be viewed as a call, and there are those who, like me, should never have married. I know the Lord hates divorce—that's in the Bible—and divorce shows that sin has been committed. But was the sin simply in the divorce, or was the sin in the marriage that should never have been? And if there has been sin, how should it be resolved? True marriage is a blending process, similar to the blending of copper and zinc to create nickel. If there has not been blending, there has not been a real marriage. Divorce is simply a legal recognition of that fact, painful though it might be."

John sees the pain of divorce as a form of penance. It is a constant reminder of the seriousness of marriage, and in this sense, at least, a kind of mercy. But at the time of his separation from Nancy, John could find no mercy. "I went through absolute brokenness. I was face down in the dirt, confronted with my own failure. It was like death. I found myself identifying in a small way with the agony of Jesus. My only comfort was to relate my sufferings to Christ in some way," he says.

"How did all of this affect your music? And what did Billy Ray Hearn have to say about this development?" I wondered.

"If you go back and look at those two first Christian albums I recorded, *John Michael Talbot* and *New Earth*, you will see that I wrote liner notes to and about Nancy. I was hoping for the best—I was optimistic. Of course, at this time we were desperately struggling with our marriage. Then we split, and I wondered what the industry would have to say about it all," John remembers. "I found Billy Ray to be a truly exceptional man within the Christian music world. He calls Sparrow Records a Christian business and says it should not only support the music ministry, but the artists as well—the *people* behind the music. When I went through my separation and divorce, he didn't write me off. He was concerned about my personal life. He wanted to know whether I would be okay. He was also concerned about Nancy and Amy. He urged me to take my time, to think things through. He approached me not only as the president of a record company, but as an elder in Christ and a true friend. He didn't attempt to tell me what to do. He was just incredibly supportive and I will never forget that."

There were others who shared John's hurt and sorrow, supporting him empathetically: Barry McGuire, Phil Keaggy, Nancy Honeytree, Mike Warnke—he now calls them his "Good Samaritans."

"There was one brother who had a nationally known music ministry and who roundly condemned me. We had been friends, but things deteriorated sharply when he learned of my separation. He said I was going to hell, that I must repent, or be damned. This didn't help my already sensitive emotional state or my badly bruised self-image. Even though it was Nancy who wanted out, I received the full wrath of this particular individual. He was very well-known around the country and immensely talented. I tried to make peace with him before his untimely death in an accident, but it didn't happen," John sighs.

Deeply aware of his own sin and failure, John nevertheless continued to cling to the treasure of his salvation—his vision of Christ still alive in his memory. It was his only consolation—his inner island of calm in the midst of the hurricane that rampaged through his soul. But there seemed to be no promise of a fresh beginning, no energy left to start all over again. The public ministry would have to go—maybe even the music. He would lay it all down at the feet of the crucified Christ before wandering into the desert to seek the path on which he was to walk. He would, he thought, simply withdraw to his own corner of the universe, praying that somehow God would find him useful in some small way.

It was then that he met Father Martin.

Chapter Six

Tracking the Path of Saint Francis

He had worked at his craft for a decade, since the age of ten. Calloused fingers and many hand-written pages of songs testified to years of diligent practice and creativity. He had managed to survive four taxing years of life on the road with Mason Proffit and had become a spokesman for a generation of young people seeking truth and justice. Having weathered many storms, he seemed to have emerged on top of things with few real scars. John Talbot's resilient spirit and raw determination had always seen him through. That is, until Nancy asked for the divorce. His world, including an extremely promising future as a Christian musician, had been turned upside down.

In the spring of 1977, feeling like a condemned man, he offered the house and nearly everything else to his wife, seeking temporary solace in the warmth of his parents' home. It was a harbor of safety, a kind of half-way house as he entered one of the most severe transitions that a man can face. Already, he missed seeing little Amy. Two years later, John wrote these words in his journal:

> I see my daughter, and my heart yearns to be a normal father for her. She loves me deeply, I love her deeply, but because of Nancy's remarriage, the reality of my being a normal day-to-day father is impossible. I see her confusion and hear her questions, and I cannot answer them. I am moved to great sorrow. Soon her

77

presence stirs a great love and great pain within us both, so that I am nearly unable to be around her and still keep my composure. I am truly sorry that this little girl must suffer from the mistakes of my youth, yet no matter how sorry I am, it seems that both she and I must suffer this separation that neither of us really wants. This is my lifelong penance I suppose, for whenever I see this little child I am unable to hold back the tears that well up within my penitent soul.

The dissolution of John's family produced a sorrow that was compounded by the uncertainty of his professional future, not to mention his frightening doubts about his spiritual journey. He needed help—he needed counsel. For someone who has enjoyed esteem in the eyes of others for so long, this can be a very difficult admission; however, a broken spirit and a contrite heart had borne the fruit of humility in John's life. He observes that the full dimensions of his conversion to Christ were really released only when he plunged into the fathomless depths of contrition created by the sense of failure he felt from his divorce.

"When I was on the road with the band, I looked around and saw that the people around me weren't happy—they didn't possess the real keys to life. And I began to deduce from my readings that there was something more to this existence, and that perhaps the peace I sought was spiritual. I was working my way into what I now recognize as the beginnings of a conversion. I would call that a conversion of attrition. It was only after the failure of my marriage that I was blessed with a contrite spirit based in a kind of godly grief—a painful yet wonderful grief," he says with irony. He was down, with nowhere else to look but straight up. He felt overwhelmed by the realization that he had broken God's heart. It was through his remorse that true conversion was perfected and completed. The gift of repentance was now his.

John was drawn to Alverna, a Franciscan retreat center only two miles from his parents' home in Indianapolis. He knew of a priest there who was reputed to be an expert marriage counselor. After reading *The Journey and the Dream*, a book by Murray Bodo on the life of Saint Francis of Assisi, John thought that a Franciscan might be able to answer a lot of his questions—even if he was a Roman Catholic.

"I had been reading about Saint Francis—about his incredible devotion to Christ and his stark, simple life that has always appealed to me. I could relate to the power of his conversion. And my other readings—books on the early church, the writings of Bernard of Clairvaux, Thomas à Kempis, Theresa of Avila, John of the Cross, and Thomas Merton—were all ministering so deeply to my spirit, yet, I was troubled because they were all Catholic! I needed some understanding, and I thought that this Franciscan priest, Father Martin Wolter, could provide it," John remembers.

But his inquiry was not without its disappointing moments. Following directions to the Alverna compound, John drove his van down the long, narrow driveway, his heart pounding in anticipation. He envisioned a modest wooden structure with habited priests prayerfully walking the grounds with heads bowed. What he actually saw as he wheeled into an expansive parking lot was something quite different.

"When I drove into the complex I was appalled. Looming up in front of me was a castle—a huge stone castle circled by neatly manicured lawns and shrubs. I knocked on the door and a black woman answered. I thought, oh, no, these guys have servants as well as a mansion! I later learned she was on staff. I asked for Father Martin. Another Franciscan brother came to the door in street clothes and said he didn't know where Father Martin was. I told him I was interested in asking questions about Catholicism and Saint Francis. He informed me he couldn't be bothered now because he was fixing their air conditioning. I left very angry, as I'm sure you can imagine. What I saw was a far cry from the brown habits and modest living I read about," John explained.

But John felt God calling him back to the Franciscan center. "Ultimately, of course, I did meet Father Martin and found him to be a wonderful priest. He was in his mid-sixties but very young at heart, and extremely wise. In talking with him I found a man who understood the spirit of renewal, tradition, and how practically to live the Franciscan life in a modern world. He is a very loving, kind man."

Not only did John strike up a warm and stimulating relationship with Father Martin, but he came to know and love the other friars at Alverna, who were to become part of a new support system for him as he worked through the challenges that seemed so hopelessly overwhelming at the time.

"Tell me about yourself, John," Father Martin asked with inviting, smiling eyes that twinkled in the subdued light of his library.

"Well, I hardly know where to begin, Father." A lump filled the young man's throat as the emotional load of his current circumstances seemed to lean upon him with increased weight. He felt just a little awkward— almost as if he were at a kind of confession—but the prospect of unburdening his heart before a willing soul tipped the scales in favor of full, detailed disclosure.

"How about just beginning at the beginning," Father Martin offered.

John shared the history of his musical career, his vision, his conversion to faith in Christ, and finally the tragedy of his divorce. Numerous times he fought back the tears, but bravely and frankly he told his story to the only person he had met who seemed able to draw it all out of him in one sitting.

"John, I want you to think and pray about coming here to stay for a while," Father Martin ventured after several hours of intense conversation. "You need some space, some time to think, and a supportive environment, and you could study in the areas that interest you, such as Catholicism, community, and Franciscan spirituality."

Without a moment's hesitation John responded in the affirmative and plans were immediately made for him to lodge at Alverna. The first matter of business they would handle together involved the divorce. Then they would talk about vocation, which meant dealing with John's profession as a performing musician. This would be supplemented with a study of Roman Catholicism and church history. And, of course, they would look into the life of an eight-hundred-year-old legendary figure, Saint Francis of Assisi.

John rushed to his parents' home to pack his things, about a ten-minute job in view of the fact that he simply didn't own much anymore. It seemed he was forever giving things away. As he loaded his van, he recalled a curious dream he had had some months earlier that hadn't made a lot of sense to him at the time. In this dream he was drawn by a mysterious unseen force toward a castle in the woods. Once he was within its shadow, men cloaked in brown robes came out and surrounded him, handing him a similar garment and inviting him to stay. "We will teach you how to live," he heard the robed figures say.

As he recalled the dream in more detail, his excitement grew until he could scarcely stand it any longer. It had been from God, he concluded. It was a fantastic confirmation that he was walking on precisely the right path. He had never experienced such a novel sensation of deep comfort and high adventure simultaneously.

Once situated in his new surroundings, John felt very much a part of the Alverna family. He remembers feeling as though he were being nursed back to health by caring people. He thought of it as a kind of womblike environment, where he lived in a temporary cloister waiting to be reborn—again.

He would spend hours alone in prayer, Bible study, and reading, occasionally breaking for long refreshing walks through the nearby woods, down by a churning creek that meandered through the property. He listened to the wind rushing through the trees and took delight in feeding the squirrels and chipmunks. The place was special, almost enchanted. It is alive, he thought, with the spirit of Saint Francis, and somehow blessed of God in a unique way. There was the inexplicable feeling of home about the grounds and buildings, a sense of family among its inhabitants.

Father Martin soon set about the business of mending John's damaged ego and shattered emotions by working through the issues of the divorce in a direct but compassionate approach. "I had heard about how unyielding and judgmental the Catholic hierarchy could be on the issue of marriage and divorce, which made me a bit apprehensive. But Father Martin was so amazingly empathetic—it was as if he had endured the same thing. He had the ability to feel what I was feeling. Yet, along with his tenderness, he pointed out my shortcomings and moral responsibilities in no uncertain terms," John states. "He helped to rebuild me from the ground up. Or maybe I should say, from my heart out. It was a welcome time of healing on a very deep level for me."

Then late one night, early in the summer of 1978, John retired to his small, sparsely furnished room after an evening spent reading about the life of Saint Francis. In one corner was his thin mattress and a blanket, in another corner an old table served as a desk. Books littered the bare hardwood floor and his guitar rested against the windowsill. He lit a single candle, reclined on his bedding with his well-worn Bible in hand, and prayed, as Saint Francis might have, to find some guidance from the Scriptures to resolve his situation. The following day John made this entry in his journal:

> My wife decided to divorce me, so I was faced with a whole new life. I didn't know whether to resist her desire for divorce or to look ahead to a life on my own. I opened the Scriptures three times, after the manner of Saint Francis,

believing Jesus would honor my seeking his will in faith.

I opened first to I Corinthians 7:27, which says, "Are you bound to a wife? Then do not seek your freedom. Are you free of a wife? If so, do not go in search of one."

I opened next to Matthew 19:29, which says, "Moreover, everyone who has given up home, brothers or sisters, father or mother, wife or children or property for my sake will receive many times as much and inherit everlasting life."

I opened a third time to Matthew 10:8–10, which says, "The gift you have received give as a gift. Provide yourselves with neither gold nor silver nor copper in your belts; no traveling bag, no change of shirt, no sandals, no walking staff. The workman, after all, is worthy of his keep."

While I did not seek separation or divorce, my wife asked for both. In keeping with the message of these Scripture passages, I did not resist or judge her. All I can say is, "So be it."

It was as though the weight of the world had been lifted from him. Once and for all he could lay this issue to rest intellectually, while admitting to himself that he would bear the emotional scars of his terminated marriage for the rest of his life. It would be a penance he would readily assume.

As he prayerfully and thoughtfully considered his marital situation, John was forced to examine the *idea* of marriage in new depth—its social, emotional, physical, and sacramental dimensions. Out of his meditative prayer on the subject, he exploded with a new awareness of the mystical union between Jesus and the believer. "I began to see the *process,* the *pilgrimage,* the *development* of life in Christ. In the West we are so goal-oriented. We want it all *now.* But gestation and birth are a laborious process involving a sequence, a continuum. I began to compare marriage to this idea of union with the Messiah."

He went on to explain in more depth. "In any premarital romantic relationship we learn objective facts about our partner: color of eyes and hair, height, weight, dress, speech, and other superficial, obvious information. Then we abstract our learning phase toward that person's thoughts, their outlook on life, philosophy, political beliefs, morality, and so on. Once we have acquired this basic data, largely through discussion, we move toward a deeper communication—a physical interaction concluding with sexual union, where the partners merge into oneness. We lose ourselves in one another. We blend. We marry.

"When I applied this concept to my relationship with Christ, I suddenly understood the sacramental nature of marriage and the possibilities for deepening my Christian journey. I began to move toward a more existential, more mystical experience in Christ once I had gained basic, objective information. The possibilities for spiritual growth are absolutely unlimited! And all this grew out of thoughts surrounding my divorce," John says in amazement. "At first I was enamored with Christian ideas in the early phase of collecting information about Jesus through study and reading. Later, I sought to know the *person* of Jesus in a love relationship that grows to this day. Contemplative prayer is the form of this communication.

"And I think it's important to carry the marriage analogy even farther. The natural outgrowth of marriage is children. This is true also on a spiritual level, as we are able to draw more people to Christian faith as a consequence of our union with Jesus: this is the mystical love relationship between Christ and his church."

Today John teaches what he has learned through his meditating on marriage, and is occasionally sought out for counsel. Ironically, the lessons learned from his own divorce have kept many other marriages intact and vital.

"What about my music, Martin? I've really been thinking about laying it all down." John had studiously avoided the subject until he felt the time was right for dealing with it. There were still a number of bookings on his calendar, and his father, who was handling the dates and travel schedule, needed some answers soon. "I don't know if I can go through with those appearances."

The counselor-priest sipped his coffee and rocked in his chair with a trace of a smile on his lips. "Well, John, I can't tell you what to do. That's a decision only you can make. But I have some ideas which you may consider as advice, if you like."

"I'm ready."

"I hope so, because I believe you should think twice before hanging up your guitar. You have a very apparent gift from God in your music and it must be expressed appropriately. To quit now would be to hide the light God has given you. Remember the words of Jesus in his Sermon on the Mount: 'Let your light shine before men in such a way that they may see your good works, and glorify your Father who is in heaven.'[1]

"And there is another consideration perhaps just as important, if not more so. You may want to keep in touch with Protestant evangelical Christianity, instead of withdrawing from it. I think God has chosen you as a bridge builder, a force for unity in the tragically divided body of Christ." He paused. "It's just a thought. I don't want to push you, of course."

"How can I say so when you put it like that?" John answered.

"Just pray about it, John. The Lord will point the way."

Once he had determined that he must follow through with his scheduled performances, John went out to face the crowds once again, bolstered by a revived spirit and a routine of daily prayer. His message was simple and Christ-centered, with an emphasis on worship. He was a wandering minstrel on a mission of love, with words of hope and encouragement.

He became known for his simple appearance. He had cut his hair from its customary waist-length to his shoulders. The word was out that John Talbot was undergoing some "heavy changes." But only a few knew what they really were.

"One of my main growing concerns during this period was in regard to the church. I would go out across the land to sing in churches and was horrified at the fragmentation, the division between brothers. Every group had their own ideas about where the church was going and their own interpretation of the Bible—all different. Who was right? Someone had to be wrong. It seemed like such a scandal. I wondered where all these denominations and subdenominational entities had come from, so I began earnestly to seek answers to these ecclesiastical questions, primarily through the study of church history," John relates.

As he looked into the writings of primitive Christianity and the life of the early church he found that his anti-Catholic bias and Protestant ideas were shaken severely. His first realization was that there was an awful lot of history between the apostles and Luther, yet he had never been taught about those crucial centuries. He discovered that the most direct descendant of the early church was none other than Roman Catholicism, which traces its heritage back to the apostolic era. Once he had examined the Reformation, which fractured the church in the 1500s, he had to question his status as a Protestant. "Why should I protest?" he would ask.

What John found when he researched the archives of church history was not the contemporary Roman Catholic Church. However, he found in the early church the seed that possessed all the potential and promise of the Catholic faith we know today. One of the central features of John's faith, and what he had come to view as his final authority as an evangelical Protestant Christian, was the Bible. Now he discovered that the Scriptures were not even codified into what we now call our Bible until several hundred years after Christ, through a process of canonization which, from time to time, included different groups of writings until the present configuration evolved. This took place within the Catholic Church.

"My questions of authority were really answered as I looked at the formation of the Scriptures," John states. "The authority of the Scriptures was established by the God-given living authority of the early church, through its hierarchy, its worship, and its life-style. God's own authority had established the authority of the church. So the authority of the Scriptures comes from the authority of the church—and not the other way around, as many believe. If we negate the authority of the very church that authorized the Bible, we negate also the authority of the Bible itself. I recognized that most fundamentalists and evangelicals see the Bible as their 'final authority' while denying the authority of the Catholic Church, which gave us the Scriptures. The result, of course, is that they unknowingly end up denying the very authority of the Bible that they are trying to prove."

John also launched into a study of the early church fathers. "I found the early church to be Catholic," John asserts with conviction. "It is an undeniable historical fact. I had to start asking myself some pretty serious questions about what I would do about my findings. I was beginning to identify very strongly with the Catholic Church, which went against everything I had been raised with as a Protestant."

Then there was the important role of tradition within Catholicism. John was part of a generation that had made "tradition" a dirty word, along with other loaded terms, like "discipline," "establishment," and "patriotism." One great convert to Catholicism, the nineteenth-century English writer G. K. Chesterton, makes a strong case for the idea of tradition:

Tradition means giving votes to the most obscure of all classes, our ancestors. It is the democracy of the dead. Tradition refuses to submit to the small and arrogant oligarchy of those who merely happen to be walking about. All democrats object to men being disqualified by the accident of their birth; tradition objects to their being disqualified by the accident of death. . . . We will have the dead at our councils. The ancient Greeks voted by stones; these shall vote by tombstones.[2]

Certain questions still frightened John away from embracing the Catholic faith. What about the emphases on Mary, papal infallibility, the endless repetition of liturgical worship, purgatory, prayer to the saints, confession, and ornate sanctuaries? And then there was transubstantiation, the belief that Christ is really, physically present in the eucharist. These questions needed answering.

Over a period of time, John's hungry mind researched each question with the care of a Swiss watchmaker, and the answers he found met the demanding criteria for authenticity set by his own skepticism. What he determined was that Catholicism, with all its ritual, liturgy, tradition, and devotional practices, is Christocentric, that is, Christ at the very heart of everything. If Mary is deemed important, it is only because the fruit of her womb is far more important. If the saints are venerated, it is because of their presence with, and intercessory relationship with, the Christ of the living Scriptures. The eucharist honors not only his memory, as John had been taught in his evangelical days, but it produced his glorious presence for us, according to his words in John 6.[3] Jesus is the *living bread.* And these things obtain their value not by the capricious, arbitrary judgment of some archaic, dust-covered medieval church. They maintain their value by association; association with the crucified and risen Christ of history. In fact, John found that almost all of the seemingly complex practices and structures of the Catholic Church are rooted firmly in the simplicity of three basic concepts: the incarnation of Christ, the passion of Christ, and the giving of the Spirit of Christ to the church.

John discovered further that liturgical practices and readings are based in ancient Jewish and early church customs, all of which have some deeper meaning and are based on written and oral traditions that share an overriding concern: to communicate the redemption of mankind, thematically spanning the ages from Adam's fall to the apocalypse and man's final judgment. Furthermore, John was developing a more sacramental understanding of life, seeing God working mystically and spiritually through the signs and symbols of the whole created world, now growing into full redemption in Christ. The hidden beauty of Catholicism filled him with wonder and excitement. His mind staggered under the growing realization that this was to be his church, his home in the body of Christ.

In the midst of this profound process of spiritual enlightenment, John went to Father Martin one day and announced that he would like formally to enter the Catholic Church. Father Martin just smiled at first. He was happy with John's determination to convert, but he issued a word of caution. "John Michael, I think it would be wise to wait, and let me tell you why I think you should. You are a well-known musician. My guess is you will continue to gain in popularity around the country. But remember, these are Protestant brothers and sisters and they are going to have a load of questions for you. They will put you to the test and you must be able to answer them in love, with authority, and with understanding. Remember our three guidelines for proving our faith: it must be scripturally, historically, and philosophically consistent. This will take a bit more study."

John's heart sank for a moment, but he gladly complied with his spiritual director's suggestion. Besides, he knew there was much more to learn. He would, he thought finally, actually welcome more time for catechetical studies.

Father Martin added a parting word. "You know, John, the Catholic Church is and has always been made up of human beings who make mistakes. Take, for example the corruption of the medieval era. You can be sure there will be those who will challenge you on the basis of some of the darker chapters in Catholic history. Like God's beloved chosen people, Israel, we have sinned, we have fallen, we have been tragically unfaithful at times. But we are his—we are redeemed. So, my young friend, in the words of the Apostle Paul, I would exhort you to 'study, to show yourself approved.'"

John took heart at his mentor's words of wisdom. He would have to forge his understanding and knowledge in such a way as to articulate his faith both lovingly and incontrovertibly, compassionately and convincingly. He found that he could identify closely with those Roman centurions who are said to have converted to Judaism. They recognized the Jews to be the people of God, and Judaism to be the way of salvation. They would encounter the stumbling blocks of religious bureaucracy, temple harlots, corrupt priests, and cynical religious leaders. But through it all they saw the God of redemption, they were bathed in the baptism of the mikva, endured the pain of circumcision and faced the ridicule of their contemporaries. John felt much the same, and he drew strength from the words that God whispered quietly in his soul: "John, I want you to become a Catholic. This church has suffered, become ill, and, at times, has very nearly died, but she is my first church, and today I am breathing new life into her. You will be part of this renewal."

So he continued his formal studies for another six months, after which time he was received into the Roman Catholic Church by Father Martin and a small company of Franciscan friends and relatives on Ash Wednesday, 1978. He had come to believe that everything he had learned pointed him toward Rome. John's overwhelming experience was similar to that of Chesterton, who wrote:

It is very hard for a man to defend anything of which he is entirely convinced. It is comparatively easy when he is only partially convinced. He is partially convinced because he has found this or that proof of the thing, and he can expound it. But a man is not really convinced of a philosophic theory when he finds that *something* proves it. He is only really convinced when he finds that *everything* proves it. And the more converging reasons he finds pointing to this conviction, the more bewildered he is if asked suddenly to sum them up.[4]

John found that the whole case for Catholicism is that the case is both extremely simple and very complex. The very multiplicity of proofs, which should make his argument overwhelmingly convincing, makes it nearly impossible. This was just another of the many paradoxes he would discover along the way. It was as though a veil had fallen from his startled spiritual eyes. For so long he had viewed the Catholic "cathedral" from the outside, seeing only its cracked bricks and weather-beaten facade, totally ignorant of the wondrous beauty of its sculpted interior—a hidden treasure that now was his through the rich inheritance of his adoption by the Mother Church.

"I will never forget that day," John vows. "I was received with the rites of initiation, including baptism. My godparents, Ellen and Chuck Callahan, provided a small flask of water brought all the way from the Jordan River. It was a very moving experience."

John's parents were in attendance and watched the proceedings with great interest. Within a year they would follow their youngest child into the church. When asked whether John's experience had influenced her, Jimmie responds with an unexpected answer. "Johnny was always such an extremist—I wouldn't be budged by his enthusiasm. I suppose you could say I became a Catholic in spite of John. He left some of his theology books lying around and I began reading them. I wanted to find a church home and was convinced, after studying the origins and development of the Catholic Church, that this was it. Three months later I was confirmed."

Jimmie notes her childhood baptism by a Catholic neighbor. It seems the sacramental mark of this experience had pursued her throughout her life. Now, she says, the entire family has converted, with the exception of Terry.

And how did this experience affect big brother? "I was very happy for John," Terry says. "His Catholicism has been wonderful for him. I have always trusted him intellectually, and his experience has helped me understand a lot of things, too." Although they disagree on certain theological issues, the brothers share a relationship that serves as an ecumenical ideal, transcending old barriers and isolation by capitalizing on the central issues of their faith. They have based their relationship upon the rock of the Gospel message: Love.

"The theme of my entire ministry must be reconciliation," John states with great emphasis. "'In my house are many mansions,' Jesus said. There are many expressions of Christian faith and I will not judge any of them. Instead, we must regather, come together into a building made of living stones—the church of Jesus Christ—sharing all our marvelously diverse gifts and personalities. Yes, I believe we are one in Christ already, but we must continue to unify, to direct our hearts and minds toward reconciliation."

It was more than coincidence that John's baptism was administered on Ash Wednesday, the beginning of the forty-day Lenten period of penance, self-denial, and introspection that precedes Easter—a time for letting worldly things fall away in favor of drawing closer to Christ. Indeed, John was to follow the example of a man known as history's most penitent of all Christian pilgrims, one who would renew the church with his tears, his prayers, his songs, and his wounds, after the example of Jesus Christ himself. His name was Giovanni Francesco Bernardone; he is known more widely as Saint Francis of Assisi.

Chapter Seven

Holy Man in the Woods

Who was Saint Francis of Assisi? There can be no true understanding of John Michael Talbot's life and ministry without some insight into the one after whom John has patterned his life. It's not that John desired to displace Jesus Christ as his supreme model of faith, but rather that Saint Francis achieved, perhaps more than any other person, conformity to the image of Christ. Saint Paul urged believers to "be imitators of me, as I am of Christ," and on this principle, an international movement of Christian "imitators," the Franciscans, arose to follow the example of Saint Francis, a poor beggar dressed in rags who preached a Gospel of love that was to shake Christian Europe to its foundations.

Saint Francis is the patron saint of Italy, of animals, of ecology, and perhaps most importantly in our age of nuclear weapons, he is the patron saint of peace. He forbade his followers to bear arms. His artistic talents helped provide impetus to the Renaissance and it has been said that his "Canticle of Brother Sun" was the earliest major poem penned in the Italian language. Franciscan missionaries carried the Gospel to China, and even sailed with Columbus. Major cities, mountain ranges, rivers, and geographic regions bear his name, not to mention many great institutions around the world.

In the early 1200s, in the days of Pope Innocent III, the neighboring cities of Perugia and Assisi teetered on the brink of war. Francis, the son of wealthy cloth merchant Pietro Bernardone, was a carefree youth who graduated from partying to soldiering as hostilities between the two cities escalated. Francis's dreams of vic-

tory and glory were dashed when he was taken
prisoner. The slaughter of war, imprisonment, and a lin-
gering illness changed the young man, and, in spite of a
homecoming followed by festive celebration, Francis
was never to be the same; later he would claim it was
then that God had spoken to him. He publicly re-
nounced his previous commitment to frivolity, high living, and wealth in a radical conversion to simplicity,
poverty, and the Gospel.

Donning brown sackcloth with a length of rope for a
belt, he wandered into the countryside with nothing
save his burning drive to follow God, who had urged
him in a vision to "rebuild my church" as he was praying
before a crucifix at the ruins of the old church of San
Damiano. Taking the message to heart, Francis set about
acquiring stones with which to rebuild the fallen structure. This reconstruction project foreshadowed the spiritual revival of the Western church that Francis was to
inspire. His gentle revolution, however, would not go
unchallenged. There would be the classic "conflict between living piety and church authority, between the
enthusiasm of Pentecost and the rigidity of church law,"
as Karl Adam wrote.[1]

Francis was a societal dropout, if you will; a medieval counterculture type who wandered the continent,
preaching repentance and challenging the inflexible,
petrified Roman Catholic Church of his day with a kind
of dynamic power unheard of since the mighty wind of
the Holy Spirit had blown in Jerusalem's upper room. A
grassroots movement grew, leaving thousands wearing
the simple brown habit that had come to identify Franciscan disciples by the time Francis died.

Among the numerous charismatic gifts and miraculous signs associated with this great saint are the stig-
mata—the wounds of Christ's crucifixion—that were
emblazoned permanently on Francis's hands, feet, and
side. Francis was a man of both great joy and deep sorrow. While it is true that carefree happiness and joy
were part of Francis's life, he also entered into the

darkness and pain of Jesus' crucifixion, the marks of which he would bear for the rest of his life.

John Talbot's earliest inclinations would seem to have cast him in the role of a Franciscan long before he was ever aware that such an expression of spirituality existed. From his childhood moments of solitude in nature to the three Scripture passages that would propel him to the Franciscan Third Order, John's life is one of parallels, echoes, and images of the great troubadour himself—Saint Francis.

John is fascinated by Saint Francis's passion for simplicity. "Francis was a simple man with a simple faith. He once said 'Blessed is he who expects nothing, for he shall enjoy everything.' Simplicity and poverty may be seen to bear on the peace issue also because Francis believed that those who have possessions must also have weapons with which to defend them. This was typical of his logic. I have always longed for that kind of life—it doesn't mean that we ignore the very real complexities and responsibilities around us; it just means that *centrally* our lives are *about* the simple faith of the good news of Jesus Christ," John affirms. "The three Scripture passages that came to me very forcefully, moving me toward a truly simple lifestyle, were along the following lines: The first is the tale of the rich young man whose refusal to sell his earthly possessions occasioned the parable of the camel and the needle.[2] The second was the commandment to the disciples to take nothing with them on their journey, neither a staff, nor extra clothing, nor money.[3] The third was that to follow Christ we must also carry his cross.[4] These ideas from the Scriptures were embraced not only by me as I received them, but they were very much a part of Francis's call," he points out.

Indeed, to stand back and review the life of John Michael Talbot alongside that of Saint Francis is an intriguing exercise in seeing double. Both may be said to have lived the rags-to-riches story in reverse, and by choice. Both had tasted the fruits of worldly success, material possessions, and popularity. Certainly both individuals may be said to have had radical "Damascus Road" type conversions, followed by the initial disapproval of loved ones. The same three Scripture passages inspired their vocations, and these callings were similar in that they were poetically, lyrically, and musically oriented. Both men, while wearing habits and engaging in religious life, were really laymen prophetically addressing the church in humility, seeking its renewal. John and Francis share an immense love of nature, identifying with it as a kind of sibling under God's parenthood. Each has had a reputation for flinging himself into his work with total commitment and tenacity. And both are known for maintaining ascetical routines without being gloomy or morose. In fact, both are very celebrative. Both men, physically and figuratively, have built up the stones of the church in active lives balanced by regular periods of deep contemplative prayer.

Thus it is not surprising that John, after studying the life of Francis, should have immediately wanted to "join up." John's Franciscanization, so to speak, transpired virtually simultaneously with his Catholic conversion process. Under the watchful eye of Father Martin, he became a Third Order Secular, joining with other lay people, single or married, who wish to identify with the spirit, call, and rule of Saint Francis.

It should be noted that there are three orders of Saint Francis: the First Order, or the order of Friars Minor, are celibate, vowed men. The Second Order is comprised of cloistered nums, or "Poor Clares," as they are sometimes called, after the first Franciscan sister. The Third Order is made up of vowed and non-vowed brothers and sisters, as well as married couples, who seek to follow the example of the saint from Assisi, either in community or private homes. It is in the latter order that ripples of renewal are being felt throughout the land, as the timeliness and relevance of Francis's message strikes home in our day. John has become very much involved in this process.

Within the context of his Franciscan identity, John may be called a monk, a hermit, a religious, and a penitent, all terms that are qualified by a set of criteria long-established within the tradition of the Roman Catholic Church. A monk is a solitary (one who is called to solitude, either communal or individual). A hermit's life includes substantial, but not necessarily total, solitude and silence. The religious professes the "evangelical counsels" of poverty, chastity, and obedience, either by a vow or a promise. The penitent is a class or order of brothers or sisters living a consecrated life in the church. Penitents are not necessarily seculars or vowed religious, yet many are religious in that they profess the evangelical counsels, and a number of penitents are Secular Franciscans, which is simply a modern name for Franciscan Penitents.

While the various classes and ecclesiological terms may baffle the neophyte, it is important to think in terms of the Gospel for which Saint Francis lived and poured out his life. The central theme is to follow Christ diligently, to be conformed to his image by his call to repentance and love.

As John grappled with the Franciscan ideals at Alverna in 1978, he felt himself deeply and totally drawn, not only to Saint Francis, but to an uncompromisingly Christian community, an ideal he had held for years. As he struggled in prayer for a more focused picture of his vocational direction, it seemed that five distinct ideas, some of which had been in the back of his mind since 1972, had begun to crystalize: an agrarian-based, substantially self-supporting prayer community; a call to poverty; a commitment to celibacy; a call to enter the Catholic Church; and a visual image of an old and tattered habit. One by one, these aspects of his spiritual odyssey had taken shape and were in various stages of development. He sought the advice of Father Martin on these matters, as he considered his suitability for the First Order of Saint Francis.

"John had a lot of questions when he first came to Alverna," Father Martin remembers. "His was a somewhat unusual situation and I took great interest in him from the beginning. His attraction to the church was from two angles: his attraction to Catholicism and his zeal to know more about Saint Francis. He fit the Franciscan ideal perfectly because of his sincere desire for simplicity, poverty, and humility. John has a unique talent, special graces. He is attuned to the new flow in the church—he has an uncanny feel for the times and seasons, so to speak. He bridges the gap between Protestantism and Catholism, having tasted the best of both worlds: the born-again, emotional experience common to evangelicals, and the structured, liturgical disciplines of Catholic faith. He has heart and structure and a sense of how renewal is happening in both areas."

As John sought the wisdom of the priest regarding entry into the First Order, Father Martin advised him to move toward the Third Order instead. "The First Order is a much tighter institutionalized discipline—you'll find your wings clipped. You wouldn't be the free spirit you have been, which I feel is part of who you are," the priest cautioned during one of their many meetings.

John took to heart Father Martin's counsel and his suggestion to read about the life of Franciscan layman Raymond Lull. That this suggestion was made on the feast day of Lull added force to the idea of researching his story.

Raymond Lull was a married man who, after seeing a vision of Saint Francis, underwent a profound conversion experience with an accompanying desire to live a Franciscan life-style. After having partaken of the high life, his commitment to personal poverty and radically changed values was too much for his wife. He provided for his family's needs, lived as a hermit for a period of time, then went out to start contemplative Franciscan communities that served as training grounds for evangelists. He later took the Gospel to the Islamic world, pioneering this kind of evangelism in the Middle East, where he died. Lull became known as the prime example of Franciscan foreign missionaries, as the followers of Francis sought to take the Gospel of Jesus Christ to the four corners of the earth. Ironically, while it was the First Order friars who fulfilled this ambitious world mission, it was the Third Order, an order which some might be tempted to overlook, to which Raymond Lull belonged.

John took the advice and the example of Lull seriously and decided to become a tertiary, a Third Order Franciscan. He put on a ragged habit, walking yet another mile in his journey, fulfilling one more facet of his dream. Determining that it was time to withdraw temporarily from active life, John heeded an inner call to silence, solitude, and contemplation. He was about to embark on a trek into the wilderness to be tested, tempered, and tried.

An important decision made in those days involved music. After much agonizing and many hours of prayer, John dusted off his guitar and launched a revived musical career. After having put Sparrow Records on hold following his first two Christian albums, he called Billy Ray Hearn to push ahead with an ambitious new project. Using the Catholic mass, and particularly the Eucharist, as central themes, he wrote and recorded what was eventually to become his biggest-selling album to date, *The Lord's Supper.* He had given it all up, but God was about to deal it back to him. The album was a huge hit among Protestants and Catholics across the nation. After having made a promise to live in poverty, John's royalties would reach six figures.

What would he do with the money? How could he offer it to the Lord? Memories of Eureka Springs danced through his mind and his excitement rose.

Before a new dream could be realized, however, there was a more pressing matter—his desire to experience the rigors of the life of silence and solitude. John's initial consideration, and what was probably his most conscious motivation, was his sincere desire to truly be like the very early followers of Saint Francis, who had dedicated themselves to prayer and radical simplicity.

"I was reading about their devotion, their prayer lives, and I said, 'Hey, why can't somebody just do it?' I felt an inner call to solitude—a time of separation to consider this lifestyle in more depth. I saw it as seeking and fulfilling the vision of solitude and simplicity all at once," he explained. "Just after I completed *The Lord's Supper* I retired to the woods."

But there were also other forces—unseen influences in the realm of the Spirit—that drove John to his decision to become, at least for some months, a hermit. There was within him a deep thirst for the kind of wisdom that is not obtained from mortal men. There are shades of understanding and spiritual insight that may only be acquired through the shaping of the soul in a place of barrenness and total quiet. John knew that the history of the church offers many examples of monks who braved the wilderness alone to seek the face of God and his gifts of truth, produced like pearls in the hearts of those who truly live to discover. Now he wanted to share this experience.

Saint Benedict, a sixth-century Italian monk, was such a man. In his quest for God he established a monastic movement that would become the model for nearly all monastic life in the Western church. Appropriately, he is called the father of Western monasticism. His biographer, Saint Gregory the Great, summed up Benedict's life with the phrase *soli Deo placere desiderans* ("he sought to please God alone"). Benedict's life was simple and austere.

History tells us that many have followed some form of the Benedictine Rule. John's awareness of the monastic tradition nudged him in this direction. Of some interest to him were the cenobites, or community-based monks, such as the Benedictines and Cistercians. Of primary interest were the hermits, or solitaries, such as the Carthusians. The call of the monk is, quite simply, the search for God. It is interesting to note that the earliest Franciscans were themselves hermits who mixed the contemplative life with the wandering life of the itinerant preacher. The "monastic body," according to the late Trappist monk Thomas Merton, "is held together not by human admirations and enthusiasms, which make men heroes and saints before their time, but on the sober truth, which accepts men exactly as they are in order to help them become what they ought to be."[5] This statement has the effect of putting the ideals of the monk within our grasp, and not reserved only for those spiritual giants who live alone in the cloistered cells of remote monasteries.

It seemed to John that God is not found in clamoring crowds or public places, but alone in the quietness of solitary thought and prayer. So he set about on a search for a place—a single cell or room in which he might escape the noise of the world and be captured in the grip of his God. The Scripture passage that kept ringing in his ears was in the words of Jesus himself, "Seek and you shall find; knock, and it shall be opened to you."[6]

As he walked down by the creek one day to the Shrine to Our Lady of Lourdes with its beautiful statue of Mary, John paused for a long moment. Fall was already in the air and a light mist hung just above the ground. He fixed his gaze on the mother of Jesus. Except for the babble of the brook, there was silence. What about right here, he asked himself as his eyes fell upon a likely spot near the shrine. I'll build a hermitage with my own hands, just like Francis did at San Damiano, he resolved.

He made the following entry in his journal:

I must now relate an incident that occurred on the feast day of Mary's assumption into heaven. I was walking along the ridge in the woods above the creek. I was engulfed into the being of these woods. I submerged myself in the hidden solitude to find God's presence in his creation. Soon I was led to the back of the shrine in honor of our Lady. It was there that I experienced incredible contemplative graces that surpass the mere words I would now use to describe them. It was upon this spot that I felt I had found my place of beginning. It was upon this spot that I felt I would be led to live my contemplative life in solitude.

John set about his task with single-minded perseverance, eyes riveted straight ahead to what Saint Paul called the mark of the high calling. Quietly but deliberately, he searched out the materials he would need to construct his chamber of prayer in the woods: an old barrel to serve as a woodburning stove, timbers with which to frame the structure, and stones to build it. "Like Francis," John wrote in his journal on August 24, 1978, "I will do lowly manual labor, not in exchange for money, but for the basics of food, clothing, and shelter."

Precedents for facing the ravages of temptation in the wilderness predate Saint Benedict, and even Jesus, for that matter. While they endured their fasting and solitude, the biblical prophets also sojourned in the desert, their greatest miracles of faith occurring in this stark environment. The ravens fed Elijah in the desert, and David exiled himself to the desert before ascending the throne. And long before these events, the Israelites, when called by God out of their slavery in Egypt (a type of the bondage of sin) to pass through the waters of the Red Sea (baptism) on their journey to the promised land (the completed work of redemption), spent an entire generation in the desert, where they were tested, taught, and given the Ten Commandments. The desert wilderness, it would seem clear from the pattern, is an unavoidable link between the call to conversion and the call to vocation. The difference to be found among the redeemed is that they are the ones who have sought that place with holy determination, while others try to avoid it.

When he had completed his dwelling, John closed himself up like Noah in the ark until such time as God himself would summon him forth to an active life. Entombed for months on the hillside near the statue of the

Virgin, cycles of contemplation, meditative prayer, and study were his daily lot, which also included a meager diet and an occasional walk through the woods.

"I felt as though I had been led by the Spirit into a wasteland to be tempted by the devil himself. And I was. The experiences that took place within me and within that hermitage I could never describe in words," John claims in a solemn tone of voice. "I was brutally confronted with the horror of my own sinfulness, frailty, and susceptibility to temptation. In a very real way I was forced to deal with my own humanity, my mortality. It was an awesome experience."

John was ready to live in the little hut for the rest of his life if God wanted him to. He would continue to read, write, and search out the mysteries of God. Ideas came forth as he considered his conversion and vocation, and he recorded them in his journal. Regarding concerts he wrote, "They came to hear powerful oratories and I told them of silence. They came to hear my theological explanations of the Word and I simply shared with them my relationship with the living Word." Regarding prayer, "it is the foundation of life for the contemplative"; and community, "the city of God set on the hill of this world cannot be hidden." In regard to the silent life, "I see for myself the definite possibility of contemplative life in a community of men living in solitude and silence"; concerning possessions, "my call to poverty is simply a call to the cross . . . my treasure must be only in heaven so that my heart will be only in heaven."

John's prayerful thinking was to cover other topics, such as chastity, celibacy, obedience to vocation, stability, humility, music, and the Franciscan vows he knew he would take. Vague ideas began to take on concrete form in his mind, while concrete preconceptions were dispersed into clouds of mystery. As Chesterton wrote, "The one created thing which we cannot look at is the one thing in the light of which we look at everything. Like the sun at noonday, mysticism explains everything else by the blaze of its own victorious invisibility." John discovered that mystery in and of itself is a kind of elucidation.

There were those who, upon hearing rumors about "the holy hermit in the forest," would travel long distances to seek out wisdom and counsel in John's cramped cloister. Some were priests, baring their doubts, questions, and even their souls in hours of penetrating conversation. Often John would learn as much as his visitors. As he says, "They thought there was a holy man in the woods, but it was just me."

Here John underwent a kind of interior metamorphosis that would give direction to his journey and empower him to accomplish his tasks. He envisioned a prayer community in which many concerns would be lived out, from prayer to preaching, from the arts to manual labor, from receiving the Eucharist to living out the fundamental ideals of Saint Francis.

The vision, once seen in the darkness of his enclosure, seemed to expand with the brilliance and force of a sunburst. The possibilities seemed so endless, the promise so near at hand, the answer so profoundly simple. Just like Francis.

By January 1979, John had endured the dead of winter in a frozen cubicle with only his barely adequate bedding, chair, table, lamp, and books. The chill of the air was hardly banished from the room by the primitive wood stove, which he stoked with fallen branches. He had conquered the loneliness and severe conditions. He now felt ready to reemerge with new plans forged in the stillness of a hundred prayer-filled nights.

He planned a pilgrimage to the Holy Land in February—a fitting sequel to experiences at Alverna and in the hermitage. But before he left his hillside retreat, he recorded a growing conviction in his journal: "January 1, 1979, 9:00 P.M. My heart longs for a reuniting of the people of the Christian faith . . . I believe that the eschatological regathering of Israel, foretold by the prophets, as a sign of the end times, symbolizes the regathering of the dispersed church back into her original homeland. I believe we will be substantially re-united before Jesus returns."

With this ideal in mind, John undertook an ambitious project—the writing of a volume entitled simply, *The Regathering*. The book was published in February 1981 in order to answer the deluge of letters inquiring about the thoughts of this Franciscan hermit. "In my opinion," John wrote in his introduction, "it is only by returning to this ordained, workable unity that Christianity will once more be a consistent, working manifestation of Jesus' simple truth and forgiving love. For where there is the truth of God's love, there must also be unity among God's people."[7]

A naive expectation? An impossible dream for the hopelessly divided body of Christ? Some would say so. However, the vehicle of reconciliation is often found where we least expect it. While synods, councils, and ecclesiastical task forces chaired by scholars and theologians hammer away at their meticulously worded documents from decade to decade, a gentle revolution of love and renewal is erupting around the world, bringing believers of diverse denominational persuasion face to face in fraternal fellowship. And on numerous occasions these winds of renewal have blown the young troubadour into their midst to play his music and share his dreams of a grand family reunion of all Christian brothers and sisters.

The Regathering explains Catholicism and reaches out to those who are serious about following Christ in a meaningful pilgrimage toward unity. It urges us to "respond now to the prophetic call of God."

One of the beauties of the Franciscan family is that, while it is strongly Catholic, it is also highly ecumenical in its spirit and its practice. There are participants from Protestant backgrounds, many of whom are now forming their own prayer communities around the country. "I have tremendous hopes and dreams for these communities," John states with the enthusiasm of a carpenter at work for the Master Builder.

John began his work quietly, laboring in his own little portion of God's great church. Having just emerged from silent solitude and bursting with an inner sense of purpose and direction, he looked on in near incredulity as God seemed to unfold a vast plan before him.

Chapter Eight

A Troubadour Sings New Songs

As the date of John's departure for the Middle East approached, he made the decision to abandon his self-imposed imprisonment, at least for the time being. He knew there would always be the call to solitude and that he would have to prayerfully balance active and contemplative pursuits. The hermitage experience was, in a sense, the inauguration of a cycle of action and meditation.

It seemed that God had taken this hillside tomb and turned it into a womb where the gift of music residing in John's soul was blessed with wings of flight. It would burst forth from the darkened cave with a force that would shortly be felt around the world. Indeed, this tour to the Holy Land was to be the first leg of an international itinerary that has not yet ended.

Even before he reentered the outside world, it was apparent to all that *The Lord's Supper*, recorded before his retreat, was going to be a monumentally successful record album in Christian sales outlets. It is based on the Catholic mass; although John had not yet converted at the time he wrote the music, he had been immersing himself in the liturgy as he prepared to enter the church. The unbridled excitement at something about to be encountered—in this case, John's entry into the church—is what makes this record so energizing, so charismatic.

"What prompted you to do the record in the first place, John, especially when you were questioning your musical career and about to close yourself up in the hermitage for several months?" I inquired.

"I was so inspired by the mass that I just had to write something, and because I am a musician, it came out in music. I sat down and in one day created the entire project, using my guitar and voice. It just tumbled out," he answered.

"This was a surprise record," John recounts. "After going ahead with production I took the disk to Billy Ray Hearn for evaluation. He thought it was going to be in Latin and was a bit reticent to take on the project. But when he played the record, things began to happen—people from down the hall at the Sparrow offices quickly appeared in Billy Ray's doorway wanting to know whose music it was. Some of them said it was the most beautiful music they had ever heard."

Billy Ray reluctantly signed the record into production on Birdwing, a division of Sparrow, undoubtedly wondering just how this Catholic-sounding product would be received in the predominantly Protestant book and record stores that carried Sparrow merchandise. It seemed like both a public-relations and a business gamble.

"But the fact of the matter is, it just took off from day one," John adds. "The only thing I can say about that record is that it was a gift from God. It was not just me. It was the result of a community effort. I used a good orchestra, a good producer, and a group of brothers and sisters who sang spontaneously and worshipfully in what sounds very much like a charismatic choral session.

"When Billy Ray sensed the spirit of renewal that came through loud and clear on this album, he became excited about the potential for ministry to the broader Catholic market. He undoubtedly recognized it as the Gospel of Jesus Christ, which has no labels or boundaries," John says, feeling once again the exhilaration of those days when they knew they were really onto something big. Of course, the record has gone on to touch the lives of people everywhere.

And how did brother Terry receive the new sound? "He loved it," John says. "He thought it was the best material I had ever written."

But before John had a real chance to be caught up in the attention his album had generated, he was off to the Holy Land. It would be a time of pilgrimage, and, for one who follows Jesus, a kind of homecoming. He walked the Via Dolorosa, in Jerusalem, where the Son of God stumbled under the cruel weight of a Roman instrument of torture, and visited the holy places, including Christ's tomb, and the site of his birth in Bethlehem. But perhaps most refreshing were his walks near the shore of the Sea of Galilee, where Jesus and his disciples lived, almost two thousand years ago.

It was on this trip that his vocation in music began to come forth once again very powerfully but very naturally. In a letter written to Father Martin from Jerusalem, John conveyed his feelings:

> I have enjoyed Jerusalem, but it is the countryside that brings me really close to Jesus. The small villages are very much like those of Christ's time. I have enjoyed playing my guitar in the holy chapels and villages but I think the children of the villages have enjoyed it the most. The possibilities for a truly Franciscan apostolate as a troubadour for the Lord are quite exciting in a place where both the rich and the poor reside within a stone's throw of one another.

But the excursion was not without its more sobering moments, evident in the words John wrote toward the end of the same letter:

> Never before have I seen such division and hatred. "Religion" is everywhere, but love seems so hard to find. The simplicity of the way of the cross is often forgotten, even though its geographical reminder is a part of daily life.

John visited priests, Franciscan hermits, monasteries, and many biblical sites, but the high points of his trip were Mount Tabor, the Mount of Beatitudes, and "just walking by the sea." In the changeless mountains and deserts of Palestine, John retraced the footsteps of his Master while the call to his Franciscan life-style and ministry of music continued to take shape deep within.

Back home in Alverna, John wrote of these developments in his journal:

March 29, 1979, 2:00 P.M. Since the recording of *The Lord's Supper*, my new direction in music has become a visible manifestation. My ideas concerning worship, art, entertainment, and liturgy have become reality. The trip to Israel caused me to reevaluate my entire vocation. Moving more into local ministry in the Franciscan community, in parishes and album projects is likely, plus continuing my contemplative life in a more organized fashion.

With all of this, I am truly amazed. It has all developed so quickly, and seemingly on its own. I have sought only the life of a solitary Franciscan hermit. I honestly thought that was the entire vocation for this part of my life. Then I find that just when I can begin to fulfill this contemplative call, God dumps all these other possible fulfillments of other calls right into the middle of my peaceful little hermitage. I have no choice but to follow the calls of God, if I am, in fact, professing the love of God. I continue to ask the prayers of Mary, Saint Francis, the angels, and all the saints both living and dead so that I might remain humble, simple, and obedient to love. In Jesus' name. Amen.

And well he might pray such prayers, for the hermit from Indiana was to find himself the object of increasing praise and attention from the record-buying public and the religious media. It seemed he was caught in a paradoxical bind. He sought quiet quarters and obscurity, away from lights, cameras, and crowds. The natural consequences of his call to recording, however, included increased popularity, inquiries by the press, and unyielding demand for public appearances. It was with this conflict in mind that John wrote in his journal:

April 25, 1979, 11:40 A.M. It is funny that in the time when success seems to be likely, my times of deep prayer keep calling me to a life of contemplative solitude. I cry with all my heart to be poor, and it appears I might be rich. I cry with all my heart to be despised and rejected, and it appears I will be accepted in love. I cry with all my heart to be humble and foolish, and it appears I might become a "wise man of God." All I seek is the death on the cross of Jesus, and it appears everyone is offering me only his resurrection. I am really frightened of my own frailty in this situation.

It just all seems to be happening too soon. I don't feel at all worthy or ready. I don't feel I have ever really died, so how can I possibly be resurrected? I am still a novice in Jesus. I should still be taught; I should not be teaching! I am not worthy of a place of honor as a church liturgist. I should still be learning. I don't even read music well . . . much less live a holy life!

I pray that this is not all some deplorable temptation of the devil. He knows I would refuse blatant success and fame. But by disguising his scheme in piety, Catholic piety at that, he would make it hard for me, or anyone else, to discern. I must just submit to my spiritual adviser and believe that Jesus will guide me. God honors the humble and obedient.

In essence, John was offering himself advice which, as circumstances would soon demonstrate, was both timely and full of wisdom. Within a few short months of the day he wrote this journal entry, he was on the cover of *Contemporary Christian Music* magazine and the subject of a feature article. The wall of seclusion that John had built to hold back the outside world crumbled. This was the beginning of a torrential flow of publicity that would find him written of and interviewed in newspapers and magazines (including *The Saturday Evening Post*), and on national television.

John has taken his desire for true humility so seriously that he seems totally oblivious to all the attention. Cheri White, a Catholic convert from the Assemblies of God denomination, is now a member of John's Franciscan "Little Portion" community and recalls her own amazement at John's humble attitude toward his popularity. "People seem to relate to John in one of three ways. The first group are those who see him as a kind of spiritual guide or counselor, almost as a guru. The second group are the musicians who want guidance or instruction in their musical pursuits, or who are arrangers—maybe even producers—who want John to be involved in a big project. The last and largest group are the fans, those who buy all John's records and swamp this place with mail. Because they feel a spiritual kinship with John through his music, they regard John himself as a part of their own lives. Believe it or not there are a substantial number of Mason Proffit fans who keep up with John and Terry to this day. Somehow, all this seems to just fly by John. I honestly believe he doesn't know just what a following he has."

"Johnny has no concept of his fame," his mother confirmed in the summer of 1980, as she sat in her sewing room making yet another "costume" for her son—a lightweight summer habit. I asked her why she thought this was the case. "Well, John is so intense, so deeply committed in what he does, that I just don't think he gives notoriety any real thought." John sat in the corner of the room sorting through some old photographs—he didn't appear to have heard a single word she said.

This is a refreshing contrast to the inflated egos and flamboyant promotion of personalities found not only in secular show business but, sadly, among Christian musicians and singers. One senses after having been around John that he is the genuine article—a true disciple of Christ who reluctantly accepts the spotlight as part of his task as a Franciscan troubadour. This kind of humility communicates more powerfully than promotional campaigns. There is a certain power about John's music—indeed, about his entire ministry as a Franciscan brother—that could be, in some ways, attributed to his vow of celibacy. It is from his marriage commitment to Christ, if you will, that we begin to see an enormous river of creativity surge forth, taking form as insightful lyrics, skillfully played tunes, and hundreds of pages of theological notes that will one day give rise to more books, articles, records, and performances. It is from this wellspring of inspiration that John draws forth his message to offer to a thirsty world, while the rest of us search for intimacy and relationship on a more human scale through marriage and family. The work of the celibate may be focused more completely on God, and thus may yield more fruit in its season, which certainly appears to be the case with John, particularly when we see how productive he has been since the hermitage experience. Although he spends about sixty percent of his time in prayer and study, he has managed to hammer out another half-dozen albums and has traveled tens of thousands of miles, as well as running a prayer community.

While John recognizes the benefits of celibate life for himself, he issues a word of caution. "Bonhoeffer warned that if you can't stand solitude, beware of community, and if you can't handle community, beware of solitude. I would carry that idea into human relationships by saying that if you can't handle celibacy, beware of marriage. If you can't deal with marriage, beware of celibacy. Celibacy cannot be a negative reaction against love relationships. It must be a positive embracing of a love covenant with Christ followed by an appropriate love relationship with other brothers and sisters in the church."

There is also a certain loneliness in celibacy that creates an emotional pain from which one might become creative and expressive. To this John says, "Celibates who do not admit their loneliness are only fooling themselves. Celibates are often extremely lonely people. Their task, and the key to making their celibacy work for them, is in embracing loneliness and entering that dark night of the soul, coming into union with Christ, who cried out, 'My God, my God, why hast thou forsaken me?'"

It is from the lonely inner depths of this vow, in oneness with his Savior, that John has summoned the words and melodies that transmit Gospel truth to those who have ears to hear. This commitment by John, which would be called severe or excessively harsh by many, has become in reality a tender, joyous blessing for millions who benefit from his sacrifice.

John's recent albums express his experience of life at his Franciscan prayer community. They include: *Come to the Quiet*, an expression of meditative prayer; *The Painter*, an artful collaboration with Terry depicting Jesus as a master painter with his people as the canvas; *Beginnings*, which retraces John's musical development; *For the Bride*, which communicates a delicate sense of musical ballet; *Troubadour of the Great King*, a double album with a theatrical quality commemorating the eight-hundredth anniversary of Saint Francis's birth, and *Light Eternal*, which could be characterized as high-church, neo-classical music.

John and Terry have recently reunited in the studio to create another album together, called *No Longer Strangers*. The title is take from Ephesians 2:19. It should be added that John has also begun a series of albums with a distinctly liturgical style, the first of which is entitled *Songs for Worship*.

"The new Talbot brothers album was great fun," John volunteers, lest anyone be tempted to cast him only in the mold of an eternally serious monk at constant prayer. "We spent more time giggling our way into having sore throats than we did singing in some of those sessions. We love to clown around together." And what greater model of unified faith than two real brothers who, also being brothers in the Lord, bridge the centuries-old gap between Catholic and Protestant with a single message of harmonized love?

If a single thread of continuity is to be found running through John's numerous recordings, it is the spirit of renewal. The Greek and Hebrew words for breath also mean spirit. Through the rhythmic respiration of his singing, John has touched multitudes with the Spirit of God.

He describes his call in this poem:

To share the gift of music with all;
    for the rich and the poor,
    for the healthy and the sick,
    for the young and the old,
    for the strong and the weak;
To meet people where they are,
    in the concert halls and on the streets,
    in the churches and in the bars,
    in the colleges and in the ghettos;
To never totally refuse an offer to sing because
    of money;
To never ask more money than what is offered;
To give the gift God gave in music as a gift to
    the world;
To give this gift back to God in songs of
    worship and praise;
To go forth as a troubadour for the Lord in the
    royal poverty of Jesus, sharing the riches of
    this love in the songs I sing.

Chapter Nine

Little Portion of the Ozarks

The enormity of John Talbot's potential as a solo recording artist had become apparent by mid-1979. Many who had followed the Talbot brothers through their Mason Proffit days and their transition to Christian music were pleasantly surprised to see John's familiar face on a new album cover. A few were surprised, some even troubled, by his new look—short hair and a brown habit. Slowly word reached the industry and the public that John Michael Talbot had converted to Roman Catholicism and had become a Franciscan monk. True, there were a lot of questions, but judging from the sales of his albums, there was also quite a vote of confidence. Both Catholics and Protestants claimed him as their own.

Not only did he have a lot of recording work on his post-hermitage agenda, but John had a fair amount of explaining to do in regard to his conversion and Franciscan affiliation. And, of course, there were his commitments to prayer, meditation, study, and writing, as well as his travel plans that threatened to inundate his simple Franciscan life-style. Yet it didn't seem that any of these pressing plans could be dropped.

At this point, John's desire for community became more than a pleasant dream—it became an absolute necessity. And in a very real way he was already living in community at Alverna, where he continued to develop his philosophy about this way of life. "After all," John reminds us, "when two or three are gathered in Jesus' name, you have community; in this respect, all Christians touch upon certain foundational aspects of community."

In the beginning his dream for community flowed naturally from his life of prayer. The community was to be a support group of like-minded people, a base of operation that could facilitate the various functions of a multifaceted ministry. John decided to move ahead and formally establish a community of Third Order Franciscans dedicated to prayer, to preaching the Gospel, and to following the example of Saint Francis. But it was not to be an exercise in empire building, he determined; it would be a natural development. The focus would be on contemplative prayer rather than active ministry, so that both the life and the ministry of the community would be rooted in the power of Spirit-filled prayer. And so it began.

Just as Alverna had been the site of John's Catholic-Franciscan birth, it would also be the channel through which a new community would come forth, called the Little Portion House of Prayer, established by John under the supervision of Father Martin. With its handful of lay Franciscan brothers and sisters, the community took shape at the Alverna retreat center. John began to pour himself and his earnings into this community over the next several years, in hopes of providing a model that could be replicated throughout the country as the winds of renewal produced more disciples of the movement.

John wrestled with the rule of his community, that is, how the life-style and the framework for authority and worship should take shape. The community should be primarily contemplative but also allow for active ministry, he determined. The community must incorporate flexibility in "Spirit-led living." It should also bring the call of the Friar and the Poor Clare into a working community of little brothers and sisters.

John sees the counterculture leaders of the sixties and early seventies as having asked many of the right questions concerning the bankruptcy of materialism, the problems of war and peace, the simplification of life-style, and the new directions in communal living. "The problem was that they didn't have Jesus at the center of it all, or a foundation of tradition on which to build," he says. "You could say they were doing the right thing for the wrong reasons, and now most of those experiments have died out. As Franciscans drawing on a wealth of history and models from church tradition, we have the building blocks to establish successful communities with Christ right at the center."

Indeed, with renewal sweeping the church and economic conditions becoming increasingly unpredictable, people are taking a second look at the community option; their motives range from the pragmatic to the theological. There is a desire to return to our roots, and we all know that if we go back far enough, we will come across villages and communities that provided mutual support and greater intimacy. In today's fragmented world these qualities are becoming more attractive all the time.

"A lot of what keeps people away from the idea of community," John explains, "is the simple fact that they define it too narrowly. They think that community means cramped quarters, no privacy, excessive sharing, and submitting their own identities to some overriding, big-brother-type legislation. The word 'community' doesn't necessarily have to mean proximity. It is much broader than that. It is a sharing of ideas and common values. In the case of Franciscans it is their desire to associate themselves in a way that acknowledges their common goal of following the example of Saint Francis. Paradoxically," John concludes, "serious Christian community is both more simple and much more difficult than most people would expect. This is because it involves both the grace and the responsibility of building relationships in God's love."

As John gets excited, he pulls out a pen and starts drawing diagrams. "See here? We have several concentric circles of relationship moving outward from the center, which is God. First, we relate to Him. Then, of course, we have our families and close friends, followed by our church parish, and on out to the world. Many people need a level of support between family and parish, and that's the perfect level on which to establish the Third Order Franciscan communities that have flowered from the ministry of the Little Portion."

John's proposal would knit like-minded people together while bolstering the local parish with supportive activities. He repeatedly makes the point that lay Franciscans need not wear a habit, sell all worldly belongings, or take restrictive vows. They may be married, students, business people, singles—they are only required to live according to the values of Saint Francis as far as they can within their personal circumstances.

"And remember," John reminds, "You don't have to be a Catholic to be a Franciscan. There are what we call ecumenical Franciscans in Protestant denominations." He outlines his thinking on this issue in his booklet "Franciscan Community in Today's World."[1] In another work, "Secular Franciscan Houses of Prayer,"[2] John discusses the life-style specifics of his own community and its guidelines for day-to-day operation.

On a number of occasions I visited John at Alverna and we talked for hours about his dreams for community. The daily regimen was certainly more structured than a typical American's schedule. However, I found the embryonic Little Portion House of Prayer to be much freer than one might imagine a monastic setting to be. The day centers on the three to four offices[3]—these are hallowed moments spent together in a small chapel adorned only with the typical Franciscan crucifix of San Damiano.[4] Mornings are spent in quiet study or meditation, while the more active labors of the day are left for the afternoon. Meals are taken in common and kitchen duty is a rotating responsibility.

Depending upon their status in the community, members may or may not be wearing the brown Franciscan habit. It is ironic that at a time when First Order Franciscans are abandoning their habits for street clothes, many celibate orders of lay Franciscans are putting them on.

"In wearing habits, we aren't implying that other communities like ours should be wearing them. We feel that for us they are significant," John states. "By wearing my habit I am constantly reminded of my calling, and that I am God's property. It is a sign that the world seems to need and respect."

It was not an uncommon sight to see John or one of the others stooping outside the kitchen door to feed or talk to "brother squirrel" or "brother rabbit," just like the saint from Assisi and in his spirit—the spirit of the reconciliation of all things in Christ.

The Little Portion is an eremitic community, in which solitary prayer and reflection have a high priority. The hermitage experience will always be available to members, who may periodically retreat to seek God in quiet solitude and contemplation.

"The active work we do as Franciscans is, of course, very important," John allows, "but the real focus of our ministry is prayer, and everything else must be an outflow of the relationship we have with Christ in prayer. If we guard our prayer life, then we are guarding our ministry."

John's community mandate might seem introverted, but a closer look reveals a true concern for the entire world. "I believe we are moving into a prophetic time," he asserts. "We can no longer be passive about the call to unity, nor can we ignore the great issues of our day, such as poverty, injustice, and peace. I think that if we are in an environment that is attuned to God through prayer, we will be empowered effectively to address ourselves to these international concerns."

It all sounded a bit lofty to me at first, but after observing the impact that this group of Franciscans has already had, second thoughts were in order. And after seeing the growth of the Little Portion from Alverna to Eureka Springs, I would bank on this project as a formidable spiritual force.

That's right—Eureka Springs, Arkansas—John's acreage acquired at the zenith of Mason Proffit's fame and fortune. His instincts had been right. He had purchased the site of what would ten years later become a Franciscan hermitage, the likes of which had never been seen anywhere.

In 1980, at Alverna, John felt directed by God to consider resettling the Little Portion community in Arkansas. The ideas that came forth in prayer gradually took shape, and construction was begun on ninety-seven acres of Ozark Mountain land in 1982 with the support of Little Rock's Bishop Andrew McDonald. It was a sobering venture that would involve zoning problems, design challenges, and hundreds of thousands of dollars. "Sometimes the idea of it scared me to death," John admits. "But it was a step of faith and obedience. It's incredible to see how God has provided everything—right down to an award-winning architect with an international reputation."

Architect Fay Jones, of E. Fay Jones and Associates, has been recognized for his breathtaking design of Thorncrown Chapel, a structure in the woods outside of Eureka Springs. It is characterized by its towering glass and its geometrically reinforced form that vaults dramatically skyward in harmony with the trees surrounding it.

"At first I wanted simple, inexpensive huts on the land," John says. "Then we found that we couldn't do that legally. So we determined to combine a number of concerns, including quality, simplicity, cost-effectiveness, energy efficiency, ecological harmony, and aesthetics. Fay came up with the perfect integration of all these requirements. The man is an architectural genius."

The property has a commanding view, sweeping some fifty miles. Six pyramidal domiciles, or cell-type structures, are built into the gently sloping hillside on the edge of a man-made lake, fitting in beautifully with the cedar trees. Each duplex-style dwelling houses two people. A common meeting area includes a library, a kitchen, a dining room, and a temporary chapel. Eventually a chapel will be built over the water of the lake and will be open daily to the public. It will be a twelve-sided structure rising up gracefully from the five-acre body of water. A single skylight will lift the eyes, thoughts, and hearts of worshipers toward heaven.

The individual hermitages are built partially underground, creating a cavelike feeling, and are modestly appointed. Passive solar heating cuts energy expenses and maintains an ecologically sensitive balance. "In the future," John predicts, "there will probably be guest hermitages where people can come and share in our simple life of prayer and community. We would also like to provide space for families who are interested in living the Franciscan life according to their own capacity, but this is still in the planning phase."

It was in the summer of 1982 that the Little Portion House of Prayer moved from Indianapolis to Eureka Springs. Before closing the final chapter of the Alverna experience, John sought the counsel of his friend and spiritual director.

"Father Martin," John ventured as they met together for a last time before the move, "I'm shaking in my boots. I don't want to do this—it's too big for me."

"Good," came the reply. "It's good to be afraid of what you are doing. Have a good healthy fear and know that you are just a small part of what God is really doing."

In the days leading up to the long overland drive John walked the grounds of Alverna with sadness in his heart. There was such mystery about the place, such enchantment. He could feel the years of Franciscan prayers bathe the forests and buildings. "You can feel it in the rocks, the trees, and the houses," John says wistfully. "And there is such love, such compassion, to be found there. It was the place where I was conceived as a Catholic and a Franciscan—a place where I grew and was gently nurtured under the protection of holy friars, men of God. I was mothered, guided, and cared for.

"Before leaving I walked down to the creek and visited that hand-built hermitage where I had spent so much time in prayer. I cried, and I was scared. It was difficult—like a birthing process."

The *Criterion*, an Indianapolis newspaper, wrote a four-column story on John's departure under the headline, "Indianapolis to lose a man of prayer." John had become a fixture in the area and would be missed by many.

Eventually the move was completed, with temporary housing arranged as construction of the hermitage continued. John, with Cheri White, who had become a kind of executive secretary to the Little Portion, soon set up the brothers' community and the sisters' community in Eureka Springs. Five core members eagerly anticipated the various ministries that they saw as outgrowths of their call to prayer.

John and other members of the community have frequently participated in the mass at Saint Elizabeth's, often providing music and song in a supportive role. "Each person in our community has special talents. Our outreach plans include radio production, music, drama, preaching, and dance," he says. "Like Francis, we will continue a street-level evangelism, using the arts to share the Gospel. We are particularly excited about developing artistic expressions for communicating the Gospel. The arts have long been ignored by the church, but we see a revival taking place in this area.

"There isn't going to be Bible-thumping or tract handouts. And we won't be limited geographically," he adds, referring to plans for tours to many cities to communicate their message of renewal, Franciscan spirituality, evangelism, worship, and charity.

"Funds are being raised to help people around the world, with a particular emphasis on hunger and refugee concerns," John says, his sense of social justice even more evident today than in the seventies. At the height of the 1982 war in Lebanon, John performed in a benefit concert, raising eight thousand dollars for Mercy Corps International, a Christian relief and development agency working to assist the hungry and homeless. Mercy Corps provided desperately needed medical supplies during the siege of Beirut. John is currently working with Mercy Corps to establish a specifically

Franciscan project called Franciscan Mercy Corps. As he develops this plan, he draws great strength and inspiration from Mother Teresa, whose work in India is known around the world.

John first met Mother Teresa at a conference in Fort Wayne, Indiana, on June 6, 1982, where they shared the stage and were featured in an article from which the following is excerpted:

> Two special guests commanded the attention of the audience, John Michael Talbot and Mother Teresa, of Calcutta. . . . These two personalities were distinctive in their attire and attitude. Both conveyed an impression of simplicity and a mood of serenity. Contrasts and similarities were evident to those who knew them. One was garbed in brown, a Franciscan; the other dressed in white, a Sister of Charity. One was from Indiana, the other from India. One was young, only 28; the other old, 72. One was born in Oklahoma, the other in Macedonia. One grew up outside the church, the other within. One had a wayward childhood, reminiscent of Francis of Assisi; the other a consecrated youth, similar to Saint Clare of Spoleto. One calls himself the "Troubadour of the Great King," the other a "Mother to the poorest of the poor." One is named John, after the herald of Christ; the other is named Teresa, in honor of the patron saint of missions. Though this was their first meeting, John Michael Talbot, internationally known recording artist, and Mother Teresa, Nobel Prize winner, felt an instant kinship. Both have taken with ultimate seriousness Christ's invitation to "seek first the kingdom of God, and his righteousness; and all these things shall be added unto you" (Matt. 6:33).[5]

This illustrates again the paradoxical path on which John finds himself. One day he is, in a manner of speaking, hiding in a hermitage, far from prying eyes and enveloped in solitude and quiet, while the next day he may be singing at a peace march at the United Nations or appearing with a noted personality at a public function. It follows the pattern of Francis, who found himself alternately in the presence of the pope and pauper.

But John also feels a special kindred relationship to Saint Bonaventure, a Franciscan reformer of great intellect who brought balance to the movement when it was threatened with excesses in certain areas. There is a necessary tension between the freedom of Francis and the organization of Bonaventure that John will need to maintain a disciplined equanimity if, indeed, he is to establish similar communities as part of his ongoing work. This awareness has brought John into a deeper desire to study the roots, not only of the Franciscan movement, but also of the older monastic forces that helped shape Francis's own vocation and the Franciscan communities. He sees the study and application of church history as indispensable to the mission to which he is called.

"As we look more deeply into our past, we find patterns of renewal that, contrary to being archaic voices from the past, prove to be excitingly relevant to the issues presently facing us," John explains. A 1982 trip to Ireland with Father Edd Anthony, O.F.M., greatly helped John to determine some of the forces that influenced Franciscan tradition and ministry.

"I know I'll never get to the end of discovery when it comes to the study of monasticism, history, and their relationship to our own call, but what I have learned is both helpful and incredibly interesting," John reports. "I found that in the tenth, eleventh, and twelfth centuries Irish Celtic monks passed through Italy on pilgrimages to the Holy Land, and evidently had great impact on the religious environment into which Francis was born. It was under the influence both of the Eastern desert fathers and of the pilgrim monks from the north that Francis developed a new integration of mystical prayer and Gospel poverty, allowing the friars to be both itinerant wandering preachers as well as contemplatives. This, of course, led to a major renewal of faith in the thirteenth and fourteenth centuries." John speaks with the assurance of a scholar, leafing through volumes of notes and reference material as he talks—and to think he never finished high school!

He went on to explain that Franciscan missionaries had reached Ireland by 1228 A.D., a mere two years after the death of Francis of Assisi. Since that time, Franciscans have had a major impact on the people of Ireland. Remaining true to their original vision of prayer and poverty, the friars and sisters were considered holy men and women of prayer, and they were always accessible to the poor. It is easy to understand why Franciscans have always been greatly loved by the Irish.

John wants to put this same winning combination into effect at the Eureka Springs community and elsewhere. From the beer-drinking friars of Dublin to the teetotaling Baptists of the American South, from the high liturgy of Roman Catholic mass to the Pentecostal prayer service of the Protestant community churches, John sees a faith unified in its central theological points and people whose hearts are set to serve the Lord in spite of cultural and traditional diversity.

"Saint Francis bridged all those gaps in his own lifetime, and so did those who followed in his humble footsteps. In a truly Christian, truly loving community, different personalities blend to create a more complete picture of Jesus," explains John. "And after all, he is the one we want to show to the entire world. This is our challenge."

Chapter Ten

The Gentle Revolution

This story of John Michael Talbot's journey has not attempted to present a comprehensive life history. Only in his late twenties, he is too young for that. It would be more accurate to say that this book has been about the Gospel, using John's pilgrimage to cast it in modern human terms. John would insist that the crux of this story is more the exemplary life of Saint Francis of Assisi than it is his own life. However, Francis would, in turn, undoubtedly defer to Christ, claiming that only he can be our supreme model for faith. Nonetheless, there are elements in the life of the modern-day troubadour that make him particularly relevant to our age.

Early in John's life, certain gifts and natural abilities were clearly discernible. He used his imagination in a theatrical context, which later became the foundation for deep faith. He sought out nature and quiet moments, which developed into a desire to find God in solitude and contemplation—to be a monk. Youthful playing with musical instruments and his joy in singing evolved into highly articulate skills, channeling his life's vocation. Many will see that it is apparent that God placed an unusual call on John's life, evident from an early age, and that this represents a somewhat rare experience. It is perhaps more true to say, however, that all of us have a unique call of God upon us, but we have sometimes failed to recognize the call or to be fully obedient to it. John's story should compel us all to examine ourselves in order to seek out those innate abilities and special gifts that uniquely mark us for our own life's work.

John's life also speaks to us of conversion—a transforming, awakening process whereby we acknowledge the lordship of Christ and inaugurate a lifelong movement toward him, with all its inevitable ups and downs. "This has to mean more than simply participating in evangelistic meetings or filling out membership cards in churches," John points out. "It must mean a total conversion toward goodness, toward God, through an ever deepening union with Christ. It means objective fact-finding and subjective yielding. It must be a whole-person experience. And I feel it is of the utmost importance that each of us, before God, deal with the important issues of faith. The Bible says that we must work out our salvation in fear and trembling. I think this means that we must grapple with the questions, examine the history, and think through the entire subject of Christian identity. I suppose you could say that conversion must be a daily choice of dying to the self and living in Christ," John adds. "It is a gradual process of coming to know God."

It is really only in coming to know God that we can, in turn, make him known. We become the image of Christ in a lost world. It is in this context that John's Franciscan lifestyle communicates so much: simplicity, sincerity, voluntary poverty, love of God and man.

In spite of his success in furthering Franciscan ideals, he feels he still falls far short. "Just look at Francis's life and see what was accomplished," he says. "By the end of his ministry there were hundreds of thousands of Franciscans who made deep, life-changing faith commitments to live a penitential Gospel life. And remember, this was all done without television, radio, or a Christian media network. This was accomplished one-to-one, at the street level. We're talking about a genuine, revolutionary movement of love grounded and rooted in prayer. I find this tremendously challenging as we continue to build our own little prayer community."

It is out of this sense of conversion and life-style commitments that ministry comes forth. It is a delicate balance of prayer and action. In the case of the Eureka Springs community, deeply rooted rhythms of prayer have given birth to extremely creative ministerial concepts that are revitalizing the place of the arts in today's church. Beyond the music recordings, there are songbooks, dramatic presentations, dance, and many other expressions of faith that not only inspire worship among Christians, but that draw the unchurched toward Christ.

"The great medieval and Renaissance works of art were centered around the Gospel and biblical scenes," John explains, "and I feel we modern Christians are long overdue in reviving the arts. This is something that has a long and powerful history within Catholicism. Just walk through the Vatican and what do you see? You see Michelangelo at his greatest, and a host of other artists immortalized through their inspired works. We know that the Franciscan movement of the thirteenth, fourteenth, and fifteenth centuries was actively involved in the liberal use of drama, dance, and music in sharing the Gospel of Jesus Christ with the world. We need to see that happening again today. I believe it will happen," John predicts.

The Catholic Church in itself has been the object of many of John's hopes and prayers. He represents new blood and zealous vitality, challenging those with ready hearts and open minds to renewal. He builds much of his case for the future upon the solid foundation of long-established tradition and devotion found in the church itself. It is part of his call to present the truths of the faith in new ways, prophetically calling the church to reexamine itself in light of its own tenets. One cannot help but be reminded of the young King Josiah, who, having ascended the throne as a youth, later rediscovered the book of the written laws of God that had somehow been lost in the very temple which it had inspired. By a reexamination of the truth already in their possession, the people initiated a sweeping reform and powerful spiritual revival that spread throughout the land.[1] Francis may be said to have done the same thing in his day, prophetically uplifting the simple Gospel of Christ in a world jaded by political religiosity and hardened hearts. John Michael Talbot is a continuation of this prophetic tradition today.

John feels that Roman Catholics could learn a lot from their evangelical Protestant brothers and sisters when it comes to revived faith. "I think we as Catholics need to understand a whole lot more of the gift that God has given to the Protestant and evangelical churches. They have such a zealous and heart-felt faith, such Christ-centered personal commitments. And we Catholics have much to share with our Protestant friends about the beauty of liturgical worship and the historically transmitted dimensions of our traditional faith. I think we are learning and sharing with one another already—I've seen evidence of it in my travels.

"I believe we'll find unity one day—at least a significant measure of it. But this, in my opinion, will only come through a full philosophical, historical, and scriptural unity. This is the tripod on which a unified church must stand. If any one leg is removed, it will collapse," John asserts.

This goal of unity is part of the cause that has resided with John throughout his life. There has always been an ideal for which he strives, an issue to be championed. Such problems of our day as world hunger and peace have always occupied important places within the Franciscan tradition, and these are areas to which John and his community are now seeking to address themselves. They are concerns about which we will hear more from this Franciscan troubadour, perhaps in a record album, in a stage play, or maybe in a poem.

Until such time as his visions of Christian unity and renewal have been realized, John and his prayer community will simply persist in their call to simplicity and prayer. "We will root ourselves in prayer and contemplation," he vows. "We will root ourselves in mystical union with Christ. We will remain sensitive to the workings and the leading of the Spirit of God in our lives. If we do these things and listen in the stillness of our own spirits, we will hear his words of guidance. And we will go where he leads us."

John hastens to round out his message with the admonition that we take care not to run out with stars in our eyes, shedding street clothes in favor of a habit, but that we count the cost of taking up our crosses daily to follow Jesus.

As John looks ahead to the future, he sees unlimited opportunities in the Little Portion House of Prayer Associate Program for those who are serious about their commitments to Christ, community, and Franciscan ideals. "Obviously there are physical limitations on the number of people we can house at our Eureka Springs community," he says. "We are beginning to see the exciting possibility for establishing other hermitages around the world for celibate Franciscan contemplatives called to monastic life. Yet even if more space were available, not everyone is meant to tackle the rigors of isolated, celibate, monastic life. The question has been this: How might we involve lay people with our community? Thousands have expressed great interest in somehow relating to us."

Because he recognized that isolated Franciscan enthusiasts rarely had a local support group to join, John conceived of a plan whereby membership in the Little Portion could be granted on an associate basis. Whether celibate, single, or married, the individuals in the association would take the seven covenant promises of the Little Portion and live them according to their own vocational circumstances. "We already have at least fifty associates from satellite covenant communities and families around the country," John says.

John received official approval for this project from Father David Ecklecamp, O.F.M., who is the national spiritual assistant for the Secular Franciscans of the Order of Friars Minor Obedience. Father Ecklecamp is also the executive secretary of the English-Speaking Conference of the Provincial Ministers of the Order of Friars Minor. He has ruled that Roman Catholics may become legitimate Franciscan associates of the Little Portion House of Prayer and that Protestants may become ecumenical Franciscan members, opening the door to virtually all interested parties.

"This is where we will see a microcosm of true catholic unity—and by 'catholic' I mean truly universal!" John exclaims. "The associates will include celibates and marrieds, Catholics and Protestants, brothers and sisters called by God to live by the Little Portion Rule, subscribing to the seven covenant promises: poverty, chastity, obedience, penance, prayer, substantial solitude, and substantial silence. Associates will stay where they are currently living, going about their daily lives but identified with us and growing in their Franciscan consciousness."

John explained three main points that serve as guidelines: *prayer*, with contemplative and charismatic integration, along with a more sacramental approach to the arts; *study*, with an emphasis on the early church, mutual respect in sharing theological differences, and increased understanding of the creeds and orthodox teachings of the church; *life-style*, incorporating Franciscan simplicity along with material and spiritual poverty. Channels of communication would, of course, be maintained between associate members and the Eureka Springs community, creating a vibrant, pulsating network around the nation.

"If what I feel in my spirit actually comes about," John speculates, "we will see a revolution within the church, the effects of which will be felt by the world as well. The time is right." John the visionary speaks with conviction.

It is at this point that we must look to the pages of *The Little Flowers of Saint Francis*, the most widely read book about Saint Francis, written by an Italian Franciscan about one hundred years after Francis died. There is a startlingly prophetic passage predicting a massive reform and purge of the Franciscan order. The terms are very graphic and powerful. Following the downfall of the order as it had once existed, the writings indicate that a renewed Franciscan movement would spring forth like a tree from the ground by the work of the Holy Spirit, who "will choose uneducated youths and simple, plain persons who are looked down upon

. . . the Spirit of Christ will select them and fill them with holy fear and a very pure love of Christ."[2]

Yet another chilling prophecy is found in the "New Fioretti," another collection of Franciscan writings from the thirteenth to the seventeenth centuries. Francis is said to have shouted, "The time is at hand when a friar will throw off his habit . . . and return to the world. And a worldling shall pick it up and go with them into the desert."[3]

No wonder John and others like him feel themselves caught up in something enormously exciting and far-reaching. The implications for John's prayer community are obvious: renewal and reform of the Franciscan community, renewal of the Catholic Church, and increased ecumenical growth in the unity called forth by the Gospel of Jesus Christ. The Little Portion will occupy a place of real significance in the fulfillment of these centuries-old Franciscan prophecies. The members of the community see themselves as just a "little portion," but a very significant part of God's growing kingdom on earth.

"I've never said this is an easy way of life. It is not. Life in this hermitage is demanding and requires discipline and sacrifice," he warns. "I don't want people to get an overly romanticized concept of our little Franciscan prayer community. And in the midst of our growing reputation and successes, it is extremely important that we never lose sight of who we really are. We are simple dust, mere vessels of clay, with the undeserved breath of life imparted to us by God's grace. We have all sinned—God knows I've done my share. If we can just remember this, we will remain humble before our God, and in our weakness he will be made strong. I think the essence of what I am saying is best communicated in the well-known prayer of Saint Francis. Maybe that's how you should end the book."

I agreed.

Lord, make me an instrument of your peace.
Where there is hatred, let me sow love.

Where there is injury, pardon.
Where there is doubt, faith.
Where there is despair, hope.
Where there is darkness, light.
Where there is sadness, joy.

O Divine Master, grant that I may not so
   much seek
To be consoled, as to console,
To be understood, as to understand,
To be loved, as to love.

For it is in giving, that we receive,
It is in pardoning, that we are pardoned,
It is in dying, that we are born to eternal life.

Appendix

JOHN MICHAEL TALBOT DISCOGRAPHY
(with Sparrow Records)

1972 *Reborn* (The Talbot Brothers)

Rereleased in 1976, this is a well-produced and award-winning collection of folk/country/rock songs with a Christian theme. (Easy to Slip, Comin' Home to Jesus, In My Dreams, And the Time, Trail of Tears, Over Jordan, Come and Gone, Over Again, Carnival Balloon, Hear You Callin')

1976 *John Michael Talbot*

A solo album in many ways, John sings original, forthright lyrics and plays all the instruments in folk/rock and ballad settings, calling the church to deeper commitment. (He Is Risen, Jerusalem, How Long? Would You Crucify Him? Woman, Greenwood Suite, Hallelu)

1976 *Firewind* (Music & lyrics by Terry Talbot, John Michael Talbot and Jamie Owens-Collins)

A contemporary dramatic musical based on the Book of Acts, chapters 1–4. Spiritually uplifting and exciting. Powerful vocals by Terry, John Michael, Barry McGuire, Anne Herring, Keith Green, Nelly Ward, and Matthew Ward. Music and script, accompaniment tape, and staging and lighting instructions are available from Sparrow Records.

1976 *The New Earth* (John Michael Talbot)

Original music and lyrics played and sung by John Michael, exhorting Christians to involvement and reconciliation of creation to the Creator. Innovative and contemporary. All vocals and instruments by John Michael, except where noted. (The Greatest 'tis Love, Shiloh, The King of Kings, Dance with Him, The Last Trumpet, Prepare Ye the Way, Cast Down Your Cares, The Coming, The New Earth, Let the People Sing Amen)

1979 *The Lord's Supper* (John Michael Talbot, Choir & Orchestra)

Majestic, yet contemporary and involving treatment of the Liturgy of the Mass. Original music that ties the knot in the marriage of structure and freedom in worship. Choral arrangement and orchestral charts available. (We Shall Stand Forgiven, Glory to God, Creed, Holy, Holy, Holy; Lord's Prayer, Communion Song, Lamb of God)

1980 *Come to the Quiet* (John Michael Talbot)

Songs evolving from personal prayer experience. A haunting and moving collection of solo voice and classical guitar with sparse but meaningful orchestration. (Gloria, Psalm 95, Psalm 51, Psalm 63, Psalm 86, Psalm 23, Peace Prayer, Peter's Canticle, Phillippians Canticle, Psalm 62, Psalm 91, Psalm 131)

1980 *The Painter* (John Michael Talbot and Terry Talbot with the London Chamber Orchestra)

An energetic and tastefully done contemporary spiritual experience centering around Jesus as the Master Painter and his people as the canvas. All vocal parts by John and Terry—suitable for multiple choir presentation. (The Greeting, Wonderful

Counsellor, The Advent Suite, Behold the Kingdom, Create in Me, Paint My Life, The Mystery, Jesus Has Come, Empty Canvas)

1980 *Beginnings* (John Michael Talbot)

Collectors will enjoy these favorites from the earlier albums *John Michael Talbot* and *The New Earth*. Designed to trace for new listeners the development of John's style as it began to point toward more recent compositions. (Would You Crucify Him? Prepare Ye The Way, Woman, Cast Down Your Cares, Hallelu, New Earth, The Suite: Greatest 'tis Love, Shiloh, King of Kings, Let the People Sing Amen)

1981 *For the Bride* (John Michael Talbot with the National Philharmonic Orchestra of London)

A brilliant and dancing celebration of the Bridegroom (Jesus Christ) and his Bride (the Church). Heavy with imagery in both lyric and orchestration. Echoes of medieval renaissance emerge in several colorful dance sequences. (PSALM 45: Ode of the Bridegroom, Wedding Dance, Ode of the Bride; THE MAGNIFICAT: Prelude of Faith, Holy is His Name; THE ANNUNCIATION: Dance of the Heavens, Gabriel's Song; SONG OF SONGS: Canticle of the Bride, Celebration Dance, Canticle of the Groom)

1982 *Troubadour of the Great King* (John Michael Talbot with the National Philharmonic Orchestra of London)

Two-record set based on the writings of Francis of Assisi and some of his favorite Scriptures. Original music that circles from classical to renaissance to romantic to impressionistic, and back again with keenly sensitive orchestration moving between sheerest poverty and opulent richness. An inspired worship album with a message. (Sunrise, All Creation Waits, Dance of Creation, How Many and Wonderful, Brother Sun and Sister Moon, Sing a New Song, Hymn to the Praises of God, The Pleiades and Orion, Lilies of the Field, Prayer for Guidance, Rebuild My Temple, Without Guile, Praises of the Virtues, Let Us Adore the Lord, My God and My All, Mount Alverna, Troubadour, Prayer Before the Cross)

1982 *Light Eternal* (John Michael Talbot with the National Philharmonic Orchestra of London)

A sensitive, mystical treatment of the mystery and power of the Incarnation. Cantata for double choir and orchestra, suitable for liturgical use. An awesome journey from darkness into Light. Choral parts and orchestral charts available. (In the Beginning, The Incarnation, The King of Kings, Eternal Light, Mercy of the Lord, Glory of the Lord, Holiness of the Lord, The Bread of Life, A Child is Born [Finale])

1983 *Songs for Worship, Vol. I* (John Michael Talbot)

First of a new series of songs for use in worship gatherings. Simple music, giving the local church musician freedom to adapt the songs to the needs of the congregation. Songbook available.

1983 *No Longer Strangers* (John Michael Talbot and Terry Talbot)

The Talbot Brothers together again with hints of the old folk, soft country-rock style, making this new compilation of Christian message/admonition songs most refreshing and exciting.

JOHN MICHAEL TALBOT SONGBOOKS
(published by Sparrow Music and
Cherry Lane Music Co., Inc.)

The Songs of John Michael Talbot
Music from the early albums, as well as from *The Lord's Supper*, *Come to the Quiet*, *The Painter*, and *Beginnings*.

The Lord's Supper
Arranged for tenor and chorus.

Light Eternal
Arranged for tenor and chorus.

The Songs of John Michael Talbot, Vol. II
Music from *Songs for Worship* and other previous materials.

Notes

Chapter 2
1. Eric Berne, M.D., *What Do You Say After You Say Hello?* (New York: Grove Press, 1972).

Chapter 3
1. From the album *Last Night I Had the Strangest Dream.* Ampex Records by John and Terry Talbot, published by Dunwich Music (ASCAP), 1971.
2. From the album *Rockfishing Crossing.* Warner Brothers Records by John and Terry Talbot, published by Flying Arrow Publishing (ASCAP), 1972.
3. Ibid.
4. From the album *Last Night I Had the Strangest Dream.*

Chapter 4
1. See John 6.
2. The mellotrone, in common use before the development of the more technically advanced synthesizer, produced a flutelike sound on a continuously looping tape. It was popularized by the Beatles' "Strawberry Fields Forever," and by the Moody Blues.

Chapter 5
1. By John Michael Talbot from the album *The Talbot Brothers: Reborn.* 1974 Warner Brothers Records, 1976 Sparrow Records International, published by Flying Arrow Publishing (ASCAP).

Chapter 6
1. Matthew 5:16.
2. G. K. Chesterton, *Orthodoxy* (New York: Doubleday, 1959), p. 48.

3. John 6:41–60.
4. Chesterton, op. cit., p. 83.

Chapter 7
1. Karl Adam, *The Spirit of Catholicism* (New York: Doubleday, 1954), p. 241.
2. Matthew 19:24.
3. Luke 9:3.
4. Matthew 10:38.
5. Thomas Merton, *The Silent Life* (New York: Farrar, Straus and Giroux, 1957), p. 47.
6. Luke 11:9.
7. G. K. Chesterton, *Orthodoxy*, p. 29.
8. John Michael Talbot, S.F.O., *The Regathering* (Indianapolis: The Little Portion House of Prayer, 1981).

Chapter 9
1. John Michael Talbot, S.F.O., "Franciscan Community in Today's World" (Alverna, Indianapolis: The Little Portion House of Prayer, 1980).
2. John Michael Talbot, S.F.O., "Secular Franciscan Houses of Prayer" (Alverna, Indianapolis: The Little Portion House of Prayer, 1980). Topics covered include purpose, prayer, study, conversion of manners, apostolic service, poverty, property, clothing, food, recreation, the hermitage, mendicancy, covenant promises, government.
3. The offices are liturgical prayers followed sequentially through a breviary, or prayer book, based upon the church calendar. This is standard practice in varying formats in all Catholic religious communities.
4. The Byzantine crucifix at the ruins of the church of San Damiano (Saint Damien) is said to have miraculously spoken to Saint Francis, urging him to rebuild the church.
5. By Duane W. H. Arnold, M.A., and C. George Fry, Ph.D., D.Min.

Chapter 10
1. II Kings 22–23.
2. St. Francis of Assisi, Writings and Early Biographies:

English Omnibus of Sources for the Life of St. Francis, edited by Marion A. Habig (Chicago: Franciscan Herald Press, 1973), pp. 1413–14.

3. Ibid., p. 1898.

Epilogue

Much has happened since the last chapters of this book were written. At the time, many of the ideas that formed the basis for the Little Portion Community were primitive and the inspirations were yet seminal. Only now, four years later, are they beginning to blossom. Lord willing, in the years ahead they will bear much fruit in the kingdom of God and do much to feed a hungry world.

The Little Portion community has continued to grow and develop both in numbers and in spirit. The brotherhood and the sisterhood have begun steps to formally establish themselves as religious communities in the church. This process is long and tedious but not impossible with the Spirit who blows like a mighty renewing wind through the church. We now also include associates who live in union with us at the hermitage according to their own leading from God. And we have a number of associates throughout the country who live in their own homes or together in households.

As communities we have more firmly established our contemplative roots in a semi-eremitical (or socially hermitical) life, while expanding the horizons of our apostolic mission. We have added more hermitage clusters (or sketes) at the Little Portion, while several of our older members have built more isolated dwellings up by the cliffs on the ridge or deep in the woods. In these we provide an environment in which to root ourselves deeply in prayer, so that the power of Jesus himself will flow through whatever we do in his name.

Ironically, as we have grown in our communal vision, the Lord has also called us back to our original roots and a reawakening of the charismatic dimension of our beginnings. When we charismatics discover the quiet depth of the contemplative life, we often tend to put the more explosive gifts of the Spirit on the shelf. But, as the old adage tell us, "If you don't use it, you will lose it," and a spirituality that is exclusively contemplative can easily degenerate into the unbiblical heresy of Quietism. So God deemed it good to literally dump a truckload of his charismatic gifts on us again. We still love contemplation and reverent liturgy, but in our common prayer times the Spirit is now free to blow into our midst like a mighty wind, stirring the gifts into a holy blaze and leading us in a direction we had not liturgically planned to go. In all this, the gifts are not worshipped. The gifts are only given to lead us into open and honest worship of the Giver.

Many of us have undertaken our "itinerant" ministry in the little mountain towns of rural Arkansas. Here we emphasize our simple ministry of presence. We do not set out with big ministerial plans or schemes that cost large sums of money to propagate and maintain. We simply go to care. We go to a town in poverty and leave with nothing except the little we are given for ourselves or that which we beg for the poor.

We do whatever is needed. If they want us to preach, sing, or do formal presentations—we will. But mostly we just visit people to share God's love. We visit shut-ins or residents of nursing homes. We knock on doors in the neighborhood, not to browbeat people with a "sales pitch" evangelism, but to simply say "we care" and are available if they need us. We pray with and for people. We smile. We greet people along the wayside. As a result of this "no agenda" ministry, we have seen many miracles and powerful manifestations of the Spirit of God. In a day when the "big is better" model of our secular world has infected even the ministries of our churches, we feel that this ministry of littleness—the simple ministry of presence—is the most important thing we do.

In the course of our various ministries we have seen a growing number of people all around the world who wish to participate in our life-style in their own local area. This has led to the development of the Franciscan Mercy Corps. This is our attempt to help raise up a gentle revolution of the Spirit that has tangible effects on the problems facing our modern world. These brothers and sisters are our co-workers, supporting our work among God's poor and joining with us in prayer for the establishment of God's kingdom. In this way they support our relief and development work in places such as Honduras, northern Africa, Pakistan, and the Philippines. We also encourage them to gather in cell groups modeled on the communal life we live at the Little Portion for weekly prayer, study, and fellowship. We hope that out of this they might also get involved in helping the poor of our own country . . . the third world within the first world. Eventually we hope to be able to draw volunteers from these Franciscan Mercy Corps cell groups to take with us overseas into the above-mentioned areas of the third world.

Of course, with all of this I have also been able to continue my public ministry through recorded music, written books, and numerous public appearances. But through it all it is the community and the work with God's poor that remain my primary focus. By God's grace we have been able to distribute and sell millions of records and books, and generate literally millions of dollars. From this we have been able to found both our Little Portion hermitage and our Franciscan Mercy Corps relief and development work.

Ultimately it is the effect we have on individual lives that makes the difference to Jesus. Jesus isn't concerned with fame or success. He is only interested in bringing his salvation to real people with real hurts, needs, and problems. It is to this that all of us at the Little Portion have dedicated our entire lives. This is all that really matters.

JOHN MICHAEL TALBOT
Little Portion
Spring 1987